ROBOTICS

Advanced Programming and Design

Kevin McCombs

Cavendish
Square
New York

Published in 2017 by Cavendish Square Publishing, LLC
243 5th Avenue, Suite 136, New York, NY 10016

CPSIA Compliance Information: Batch #CW17CSQ

All websites were available and accurate when this book was sent to press.

Library of Congress Cataloging-in-Publication Data

Names: McCombs, Kevin, author.
Title: Advanced programming and design / Kevin McCombs.
Description: New York : Cavendish Square Publishing, [2017] | Series: Robotics | Includes bibliographical references and index.
Identifiers: LCCN 2016012069 (print) | LCCN 2016023626 (ebook) | ISBN 9781502619457 (library bound) | ISBN 9781502619464 (ebook)
Subjects: LCSH: Autonomous robots--Design and construction. | Robots--Programming. | Robotics.
Classification: LCC TJ211.495 .M34 2017 (print) | LCC TJ211.495 (ebook) | DDC 629.8/92--dc23
LC record available at https://lccn.loc.gov/2016012069

Editorial Director: David McNamara
Editor: Fletcher Doyle
Copy Editor: Nathan Heidelberger
Art Director: Jeffrey Talbot
Designer: Alan Sliwinski
Production Assistant: Karol Szymczuk
Photo Research: J8 Media

The photographs in this book are used by permission and through the courtesy of: Cover Abdulselam Durdak/Anadolu Agency/Getty Images; p. 4 WENN Ltd/Alamy Stock Photo; pp. 9, 13, 17, 20, 25, 31, 34, 39, 51, 53, 64, 65, 72, 76, 82, 84, 86-87, 98, 105 Kevin McCombs; p. 26 Courtesy VEX Robotics; p. 27 3alexd/iStock/Thinkstock; p. 42 The Grand Rapids Press, Hugh Carey/AP Images; p. 45 ChristinLola/iStockphoto.com; p. 56 Jeremy Piper/AP Images;p. 63 Detchart Sukchit/Shutterstock.com; p. 68 Photofusion/UIG via Getty Images; p. 79 Alacatr/iStockphoto.com; p. 90 FashionStock.com/Shutterstock.com; pp. 93, 95 Courtesy of Andi Burt; p. 103 Cynthia Johnson/The LIFE Images Collection/Getty Images.

Printed in the United States of America

Contents

Students should be assigned jobs according to their skills at an early team meeting.

1 Dividing Duties

So you're interested in robotics and find yourself either on a team or ready to start one. Perhaps you have some experience with coding or fabrication projects, or perhaps you are here because you're ready to jump into an exciting field and gain advanced technical skills along the way. Whatever your strengths and weaknesses may be, you're going to need a team of interested compatriots to tackle the task ahead of you. This chapter will introduce what it means to be up to the challenge of designing, building, and programming a competition robot as well as the elements necessary to function as an effective team. No one person can complete all of these tasks, so it's best to figure out where your skills can best be put to use.

A robotics season is equal parts hectic and exciting. Given demanding deadlines, limited budget, and sometimes scarce access to resources, the build process will have you facing a number of daunting challenges along the way. Dean Kamen, inventor and founder of FIRST Robotics, calls building a competition robot "The hardest fun you'll ever have." With the time crunch and rapid prototyping, robotics teams function similarly to tech startup companies. In fact, many students go on to work at or start their own tech companies based on their experiences on a competition robotics team.

There are many roles to be filled in an effective team. If your team has only a few students, don't worry: some of the duties can be handled together if given proper time and attention. Likewise, if you're on a large team, this chapter will help you sort out where you fit in the equation and what your contribution will be to the project at hand.

Robot Technician

Robot technicians account for the majority of robot assembly and, as such, rely on a number of fabrication skills to be successful. Team members in this role generally excel in practical applications and working with their hands. An effective technician may have experience with manual machine operation, power tools, hand tools, wiring, **crimping**, and **soldering**, among many other skills. Perhaps most important is a technician's ability to both accurately and precisely use measuring tools to fabricate robot components. The old adage "measure twice, cut once" applies heavily to these team members as they are expected to produce quality parts for the construction of the robot.

Technicians also require good organizational skills to ensure a safe and controlled build environment. Anyone around tools and machine equipment should wear safety glasses and closed-toe shoes (ideally steel toe) and make sure any loose clothing is properly managed. Robot technicians enforce these guidelines for the rest of the team along with team **mentors** and should understand safety as the primary concern of any project. An organized shop or build space promotes efficient robot construction and reduces the risks associated with clutter and heavy machinery.

In addition, technicians are responsible for the construction of testing apparatuses, robot field components, and peripherals like the driver control station. Even when not working directly on the robot, they play a critical role in the realization of team goals and benchmarks. Without field components built to specification, a team will not be able to accurately test their robot in the environment in which it is expected to compete. Creative technicians will also strive to solve problems outside the scope of the game challenge. For instance, robot transportation is an important factor both at competitions and demonstrations. A well-made, eye-catching cart can make all the difference when taking the robot out into the community to show off the accomplishments of the team.

3-D Modeling and CAD Users

Team members who specialize in 3-D modeling and **CAD** (computer-aided design) software use their skills to design robotic systems and run simulations to test design theories. By understanding professional software such as Autodesk Inventor, Solidworks, and NX, CAD users have access to incredibly powerful computation in three dimensions. Not all parts have to be designed in a computer first to find their place on a robot. CAD software can also be used to keep track of space and weight requirements for components if they are measured and modeled accordingly. This can be immensely helpful for determining a robot's **center of gravity** or for identifying potential failure points in construction.

The role of the 3-D modeler is to promote good design principles and provide documentation and analysis of the robot. A well-done CAD model can serve as a blueprint for the construction of assemblies and systems. In more advanced applications, the CAD user can even design machining instructions for **CNC** (computerized numerical control) devices to make parts. Some teams with high-level design teams can manufacture parts with the utmost precision by using software in this way. It is very important for design teams to have good communication with the robot technicians that ultimately realize their work on the robot. These two groups will often reach compromises between what is desired by a certain design and what is possible to actually construct.

Welder

Where the technician rises to the general challenges of building the robot, the welder specializes in the construction of robot frames and fixtures that require permanent bonding. When nuts and bolts are not enough to guarantee the rigidity of a junction, welders step in to melt pieces of metal together using high-heat or high-voltage equipment. **Welding** requires a steady hand and fine motor skills to produce strong bonds between pieces.

A student shows a steady hand while TIG welding on an aluminum robot frame. Welding provides strong bonds.

When watching or using welding equipment, team members must use a UV protective face shield. The arc of a welder is so bright that it can cause eye damage from prolonged exposure. The shield also protects the face from potential white-hot metal spatter. Pieces that have been recently welded will be dangerously hot, so tongs and heavy leather gloves are also required for any welding operation. Welders usually keep a bucket of water in which to douse pieces and cool them after they've been worked on.

Welders also regularly utilize grinding and cutting tools to prepare or finish a job. A welded surface will have a raised joint or "bead" which can be undesirable for certain tolerances. Grinding can reduce the size of the bead, but will compromise the strength of the weld, so it should be used sparingly on critical junctions. A good welder strives to maximize the structural integrity and robustness of the robot.

Programmer

The programmers on a robotics team are responsible for the autonomy and control systems of the robot. Using languages like Java, RobotC, LabVIEW, and Python, programmers interface with robot hardware to create movement and automation. Programmers excel in logical thinking strategies and are proficient in using computers. In order to achieve the goal of good robot control, programmers use all the sensors and inputs of the robot to produce a desired output. In other words,

MAKE NOTE OF IT

Simplicity and efficiency are both virtues of programming, and well-written code will be easy to read and well documented. Documentation is done with notations within the program, and it's there to tell others what the purpose of each function is and what each variable is used for. This is vital for communication if more than one person is programming.

the more information the robot has access to in the code, the more it will be able to navigate challenges on the field.

The programmer's task is to understand the capabilities of the robot's mechanical components and produce algorithms that make movements fluid and effective. As a result, the programming team must also be in good contact with the construction and design team to better understand what they have to work with. For example, a solid understanding of the drivetrain system of a robot will better inform a programmer on how to issue drive commands in the code. This relationship is paramount to the efficacy of an entire robotic system. A robot that is well conceived and constructed but lacks control will fail to perform as intended.

Website and Animation Team

It is important for robotics teams to have websites for a multitude of reasons. The web development and animation team provides the team with infrastructure for communication and planning, community outreach, and public showcasing of team accomplishments. Similar to the programming team, the website team uses languages like Java, Python, HTML, and SQL to tackle the challenges of a robotics season. This group creates a domain where all the team members may log in to discuss schedules, design, and strategy, among other topics. A website that is streamlined and easy to use will increase team efficiency and workflow by helping to orchestrate the various subgroups of a team.

It is also common for teams to demonstrate their robot with animations to illustrate various capabilities. A good animation can help to more clearly explain robotic systems or mechanisms, allowing the team to communicate their ideas and designs to the community. These animations promote understanding and involvement in robotics because they can simplify complex mechanisms and give insight into a team's design process.

Team Leadership

A high-functioning robotics team relies on strong leaders who have a knack for coordinating project goals. A good team leader rallies fellow students to rise to the rigorous schedule of a build season. With the clock ticking and competitions approaching, team leaders make sure that all of the subgroups on the team are on the same page in order to make a top-tier robot.

However, a noteworthy team also understands that robotics *isn't all just about the robot.* There are many other aspects that are critical to the success of the season which must be spearheaded by the team leaders. Team spirit is the name of the game during the competition. Leaders will work hard with other members to create banners, shirts, buttons, etc., to show their pride as they watch their robot compete. Robotics events are electrifying, not least because of the excitement of the crowd, the team chants, and the creative support of all members involved. If they show their team spirit correctly, students and mentors will have a hoarse voice the day after a competition.

Showing your team spirit at a competition is necessary for both the students and their family members and friends.

After the competition season is over, teams need leaders to organize fundraisers and community outreach events. Part of the wonder of a robotics team is in its ability to inspire other students and community members at demonstrations. An opportunity in which an elementary schooler gets to drive the robot at an outreach event could get them thinking about paths and careers they never imagined. Just as the course of a season can change the life goals and aspirations of team members, so too can the team give that spark back to the community.

Mentors

Simply put, robots are built with the dedication of volunteer mentorship. Whether a team's mentors consist of teachers, engineers, scientists, or parents, their experience and supervision provides important insight into all matters on a robotics team. With the help of a mentor, a student can learn how to program, weld, operate machinery, build websites, and design robotic systems. It's important to note that these are all skills that students can use to eventually make a living or continue research in that field. Perhaps most important is that mentors teach these skills on a *voluntary* basis. Robotics teams are incredible incubators for real world skills, and it's the role of the mentor to guide students along the path of their chosen roles. It is not the mentor's job to manage behavior or keep the peace on the team. Rather, it is their job to provide skills and knowledge for passionate students who want to build competition robots. As such, mentors deserve the utmost respect and admiration as part of the team.

Summary

So far, we have briefly outlined what it takes to populate a team of robot builders. Intimidated? Don't be. The challenge is part of the fun. People of any background can find their place on a robotics team and contribute greatly to the success of the team. If you've ever struggled in math or science, don't be discouraged: this could be an opportunity where you finally see how those subjects can apply to your life and your goals. In the following chapters, we will go into more detail about various aspects of a build season to help you feel confident in moving forward. By the end of a season, you will have learned much and hopefully gained some valuable skills that can be applied toward the rest of your life in engineering or otherwise.

A robot lifting two allied robots to score points at a competition.

2 An Introduction to Robot Design

You now have a team of students and mentors and you're ready to dive into the robotics season. From here, it's time to focus on the design of the robot and the action plan needed to make that design a reality. This chapter will focus on the process of strategizing, designing, and documenting your robot build. By outlining a couple of popular mechanisms, this chapter should help grease the wheels of the design process. That being said, there is a lot of good in-depth information on some of these mechanisms, so use this section as somewhat of a template to guide further research in your design. In fact, of the many resources out there to get you started on the design of robotic assemblies, perhaps one of the most important is the work of other teams from their many years of competing. Knowing what designs have been successful in the past can give your team a better picture of what kinds of mechanisms and strategies will rise to the top for this year's game challenges.

Before you get started on actually building the robot, you have to come up with an effective strategy for how to play the game. Having a unified strategy will help your team be able to plan out the entire season in terms of design and construction to meet goals of varying importance. Having a solid idea of which mechanisms have priority for the function of the robot will help to ensure that your robot is ready to drive by the time the competition rolls around.

At the Strategy Meeting

The first team meeting after receiving the game challenge should be centered around how your team wants to play. Before even setting foot in this meeting, team members should have gone over the game rules with a fine-toothed comb. Good robot strategies come directly from a solid understanding of what is allowed and disallowed in a given challenge. This first strategy meeting should *not* focus on what mechanisms or designs will achieve certain goals. Instead, the meeting should produce an outline for the kinds of tasks that the robot needs to perform in order to execute a given strategy. The design phase ultimately needs a big picture to work from, and it stems from a collective decision from the team to play the game in a certain way.

So what makes for a good strategy? While robot games can vary drastically in the types of challenges they pose, each one can be condensed into a couple of strategic principles. To some extent, almost any kind of game has elements of offense, defense, cooperation (in team games), and compromise. Without even knowing the specifics of the game, you can model every strategy meeting off of these principles.

Offense

Make a list of all the possible ways to score points. Your team should be able to calculate theoretical maximums for each way of scoring. If there is a time limit, you can make estimates or assumptions for how long you expect it will take the robot to perform each task. Try making a table with this information so it clearly outlines which ways of scoring look the most advantageous. This could be an Excel spreadsheet or even just a table on a whiteboard. Are you more confident in your team's ability to score in certain ways than others? Identify which offensive strategies come with greater potential risk of failure or inconsistency. This should produce a fairly exhaustive list of pros and cons for various scoring methods. Sometimes the best strategies center around robots performing low risk tasks consistently and effectively. If your robot can reliably score lower level point values, it will often perform better than robots which aim for high risk and high reward.

Are there ways of scoring points that are close together on the field? Are there challenges which can be completed by the same kind of mechanism? These factors should also influence the team's strategic decisions. Good robot designs often consolidate various challenges into singular mechanisms. This is reflected by a good robot strategy to take on similar tasks with given limitations on the robot's size, weight, and/or power.

Defense

What ways are there to try to effectively prevent an opponent from scoring? Robot game rules are usually very strict about what is allowed in terms of defense, so be sure to buff up on the penalty section of the manual. Similar to the way the offensive points can be outlined, your team can make a table of the allowed defensive methods. While this planning can be a bit more abstract without the knowledge of the opposing robots' scoring capabilities, you should still be able to make some valuable estimates of scoring prevention based on your understanding of how the game *could* be played. Another list of pros and cons should be produced in order to identify how many scoring opportunities could be limited, as well as their likelihood of occurring in a game. If the game includes a finite number of scoring materials, a robot could limit an opponent's access on the field. Moreover, if the scoring elements are generally scarce, defensive strategies could become even more effective given that your allied robots will also be competing

Teams playing tenacious defense in the heat of a match, helping allied robots compete for scarce resources.

for the very same resources. This is to say that your team's robot could fill a strategic role in a team game by identifying the need for defensive posturing.

At competitions, defensively inclined robots are usually far fewer in numbers than scoring robots. While it certainly makes sense to assert that the way to win a game is to score the highest number of points, the small handful of defensive robots will frequently fare better at competition for their ability to ensure that the score of their alliance is greater than that of their opponents. It may seem a cliché, but the saying that "sometimes the best offense is a good defense" applies just as heavily to competition robotics as it does to any sport.

Cooperation

This next section only applies to team games but is very important to a successful strategy. Due to the fact that all playing fields have a finite number of ways to score points, it can be helpful to identify the ways in which your team could be going for the same points as your allies. If you think that a scoring strategy could be unique or unusual, it could make your team a more effective ally by balancing the ways the alliance scores points as a whole. Having a successful run at competition is as much about your robot's ability to complement a team as it is about the individual skill at playing the game.

Robotics games also regularly have challenges that promote or even reward team cooperation. These challenges sometimes even yield higher point values due to their required orchestration and teamwork. This fact could be crucial in a discussion of strategy. While it would have already been outlined in the offensive ways of scoring, this element deserves special emphasis because of its importance in the scope of an entire competition. Even if a team-oriented strategy seems unlikely to score points when not paired with other teams that can take advantage of it, your robot will absolutely be noticed for its capabilities. This can be critical when top-scoring teams are asked to select their alliance partners for elimination matches. Simply put, the entire *alliance* that has the superior strategy will be more likely to achieve victory on the playing field.

Compromise

By the end of this process of outlining various strategies for offense, defense, and cooperation, your team will have some decisions to make. The reality of any robotics game is that, given a limited amount of time, no single robot should be able to do it all. As a result, your team needs to decide what balance to strike between the aforementioned strategic elements of the game. This will often mean that the team must compromise between strategies based on what they think can be achieved in a season. While this is not about crushing dreams for making the "perfect" robot, it is important to keep goals and expectations realistic in this phase. Come together and think critically about what can be done in the span of a single round. There's never really a "right" answer to this process, so compromises will be made.

It is important to note, however, that creative strategies and solutions should be given serious consideration even if they seem less likely to succeed at the outset. If your team decides that a certain strategy is impossible, there will almost always be a team at competition that not only figured out how to do it, but did it well. This fact is evident in some of the world's most innovative engineering companies. The NASA engineer who came up with the Skycrane Mars rover deployment method claims that "NASA wants an idea that everyone at the table will think is ridiculous or impossible." After all, what is innovation but doing something other people previously thought was impossible?

The Design Process Begins

Now that your team has settled on the types of tasks the robot will be expected to perform, you can start the brainstorming process for coming up with the right mechanisms to get the job done. Due to the fact that there is a huge range of game types and a correspondingly huge number of ways to mechanically play those games, our goal in this section is to cast a wide net for the kinds of systems your team should be familiar with. Be sure to keep in mind that this list is far from exhaustive and that there are almost unlimited ways of applying these designs to solve engineering problems. So let's look at some of the more popular mechanisms for competition robots.

The Arm

When most people think about robots, a mechanical claw is often one of the first things that comes to their minds. Iconic robots like those used in automobile manufacturing utilize movement in multiple axes to perform a range of complex tasks. While not every robotic arm has the range of motion necessary for high-level manufacturing, they all share the design concept of using mechanical rotation to move sections of fixed armature into position. By thinking carefully about the pivots and axes that will help your robot perform a certain task, your team can implement a claw or grabber at the end of a mechanical arm.

Motors are a very common driver of arms and claws. Motors on their own, however, generally lack sufficient **torque** to do any kind of serious lifting. Moreover, motors move too quickly to be precise when unaided by other design elements. As a result, you'll want to look into an appropriate **gear ratio** to decrease rotational velocity and increase torque. A gear ratio is the ratio of a gear's diameter in relation to others. If a 3-inch (7.6-centimeter) diameter gear attached to a motor is driving a 9-inch (22.8 cm) diameter gear attached to an arm pivot, the ratio will be 1:3. This means that for every rotation of the motor, the arm will only move 120 degrees, or one-third of a rotation. This gives the robot more control and, more importantly, more torque. In order to get gear ratios on robotic arms, it is common to use a toothed belt or chain to connect two gears separated by the length of the arm.

You can also control an arm and claw assembly without motors. Using a **pneumatic actuator**, linear motion can be translated into rotational motion via two pivot points. If the end of the actuator is secured to a free spinning shaft and the "elbow" of the arm is also a freely pivoting joint, then the arm will raise to an angle determined by the size of the actuator.

Multiple pivots allow this arm to score on tall goals while remaining a good distance from the goals.

This method can make for a very sturdy arm structure capable of lifting heavy loads.

For some more advanced arm design, try getting one motor or actuator to control multiple pivot points, or "elbows." What would happen if you were to attach another gear or linkage to a segment connected to the end of the one that rotates? Using the same shaft as the first pivot, we can attach another gear and belt segment. Something's different here, though. The shaft will be rotating in the opposite direction as the motor and driving gear at the front of the system. As a result, this new linkage will rotate in the opposite direction as the first, forming a kind of Z shape. Note that this new gear assembly also needs to have a gear ratio less than 1:1 to get any kind of vertical extension above the previous version. This is because this section of the arm needs to unfold more slowly than the primary section in order to be at an angle that's not simply complementary to the primary arm angle.

Lifting Mechanisms

Rack and pinion assemblies turn rotational motion into linear motion. A rack is like a gear that's been flattened so that you have a line of teeth. If you rotate a gear called a pinion gear on these teeth, one of two things could happen. If the pinion gear/motor is fixed, the rack will move linearly according to the direction of the rotation. Likewise, if the rack is fixed, the pinion gear assembly will move along the rack. This is useful when considering how to get vertical lift from motors that move rotationally. Rack and pinion assemblies

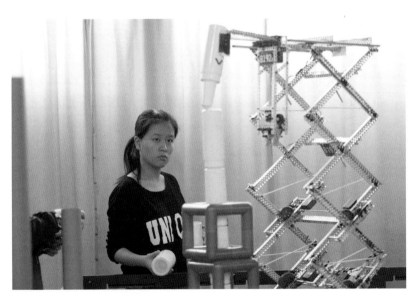

This scissor lift is being driven by pinion gears.

The flat section of teeth on the rack meshes with the pinion gear to create linear motion.

can also have multiple stages if necessary. This is perhaps less recommended than other methods for getting higher lift because it requires use of multiple motors to handle each stage. Moreover, any motor needs to be wired, so the wiring needs to be able to reach the same height as the topmost pinion gear assembly without risk of entanglement on the way down.

An **elevator lift** or belt-driven lift mechanism is also an effective method of lifting objects or game pieces. Actual elevators ride on cable mechanisms with a series of pulleys and **winch** motors. Just the same, your robot could make use of cables or belts to lift objects. Using a motor to wind cable or rope on a spool, the robot can raise a platform connected to the other end of the cable via pulleys at the top of the assembly. This will mean that the lift cannot exceed the height of the top pulley. It is possible, however, to have the elevator platform at the top of a vertical structure which is then lifted in its entirety by the winch motor. Multiple stages of this model can be produced but will need considerable reinforcement to ensure stability at its optimal height.

Scissor lifts are incredibly effective at lifting objects to significant heights while occupying a compact rest position. These mechanisms use a repeating X pattern with central pivot points as a structure. When any of the two corresponding legs of this X pattern are moved closer together, the scissor mechanism engages, triggering the same corresponding action in all other repetitions of the structure. This means that the driving element of a scissor lift is the mechanized movement of the legs together. This can be achieved with a number of subsystems. The aforementioned rack and pinion assembly can actually come in handy. When mounted horizontally instead of vertically, one of the legs can be attached to a mount on the pinion gear motor. In this example, the other leg of the X would be on a fixed pivot on the opposite side. You could, however, use two rack and pinion assemblies opposite each other to lessen the load on a single pinion gear assembly. When attempting to lift heavier loads on a scissor lift, actuators make for more powerful drivers of the mechanism. Whether mechanical or pneumatic, actuators can make use of linear motion to move the scissor without the possibility of skipping teeth on a gear or belt assembly. An actuator can also be positioned vertically on the center pivot of the scissor lift to create the same motion. Note that the legs of the X have to be able to roll or slide in a channel for this method to work.

Launching Mechanisms

There are many robot games that are centered around scoring projectiles that have been collected around the field into goals or reservoirs. Sometimes the goals are within "reach" of the robot and can be scored in with mechanisms that dump or channel game pieces. Other times, the games require that the robot fire game pieces from a good distance into scoring areas. Your robot's ability to launch a projectile certainly depends on the size and shape of the projectile, so let's go over a few possibilities.

Shooting balls may be one of the more straightforward tasks. Have you ever seen a tennis ball machine or a pitching machine? These devices are able to launch balls at high velocity and accuracy by spinning one or more rollers that make contact with the ball. They make use of friction to propel the ball by making the gap between rollers slightly smaller than the size of the uncompressed ball. This produces force on the ball in the direction that the rollers are spinning. This also means that using two rollers will require that they be spinning in opposite directions to create this force. This method excels at shooting small balls. The size of your rollers will depend on the diameter of the ball being fired.

Spheres can also be propelled out of a long tube or barrel. This method works like a cannon but without the gunpowder and combustion. In order to propel the ball from the chamber, you could use compressed air and a valve that lets out short bursts to fire projectiles. Spring-loaded mechanisms, or **spring launchers**, can produce similar results. Ever play on a pinball machine? The shaft and spring assembly acts in the same way to launch a ball from a confined channel. Bear in mind that the accuracy of this system will rely on the length of the tube used. The longer the barrel, the more precise your robot will be in hitting a target.

Mechanisms that store and suddenly release tension can also be successful launchers. A catapult or ballista uses the stored tension of ropes, springs, or simply pliable wood to launch projectiles. Instead of your team requiring the assistance of footmen to hand-crank the catapult after every launch, you could automate the process by winding the tension back down with a winch motor.

Collecting Game Variables

Robot games will often involve picking objects off the floor or collecting them from areas on the game field in order to place them in scoring zones later. Claws and arms may be effective at grabbing single objects, but for a pile of scoring pieces, we're going to need a different system. Starting with the basics, let's consider a mechanism that will allow your robot to control game pieces without letting them out. Think of machines in the real world that scoop or gather material, such as a bulldozer. Scooping mechanisms can be effective with leverage against a surface. In order to escape the limitation of needing a wall to press objects against, your robot can employ a sweeping assembly to corral objects. This assembly can be like the **rotating brush collector** on a vacuum cleaner or an extended arm that sweeps pieces toward the scoop. The rotating brush has the added benefit of keeping objects from falling out

A rotating brush collector captures a ball before it heads up the conveyor belts for collecting or launching.

in the opposite direction. Of course, spinning the motor in the opposite direction could be desirable if your robot also needs to spit the objects back out into a scoring zone.

The spinning brush technique is also similar to collecting variables with **conveyor belt** mechanisms. Using a conveyor belt with an opposing surface can channel materials effectively across your robot. Think of this mechanism like the reverse of the pitching machine–style shooter. With either a flat surface or two conveyors rotating in opposite directions, this assembly uses friction and rotational movement to move game pieces to a scoring position on the robot. These mechanisms operate better on lower speeds than the high-revolutions-per-minute shooting mechanisms of similar construction.

The Prototyping Phase

If your team has a number of mechanisms in mind for this year's set of challenges, then it's time to put some of these ideas to the test. The prototyping phase is one of the most important aspects of design as it will allow your team to test hypotheses about the behavior of mechanisms on the robot. Using the information you get from rapidly prototyping a couple of components, your team will be able to settle on a more refined idea of how the robot will actually come together. Simply put, nobody has a fully functioning design perfectly rolling around in their head. An analogous example would be like an author writing the next great American novel straight from his or her head without any revisions. It just doesn't happen like that. As a result, prototypes are like a robot's first draft. Many ideas should be tested, challenged, scrapped, and consequently improved.

Good prototyping strikes a balance between speed of construction and the ability to give an idea its proper consideration. This is the time to use low-cost materials to approximate the function of a mechanism. In this stage, cardboard, wood, PVC, and other cheap consumables are great for getting an idea into physical form. Knowing full well that the same mechanism might perform better when constructed out of aluminum, steel, or hard machined plastic, the purpose of this step is to get a proof of concept. Great ideas can work in an abstract sense, fit the rest of the robot build, and perform well in isolated tests, but can still fail when put to an actual test of the robot.

Here, it is important to try to consider all possible variables and test them accordingly to ensure that you have fairly definitive proof of a design working as intended. Moreover, prototyping should show your team the challenges that need to be overcome in settling on the eventual design of a system. Does the robot tip over when the prototype arm is fully extended? Does the shooter get stuck if more than one ball is fed into the holder? What could happen if the winch rope gets caught on other parts of the robot? These are the kinds of questions that your team should be asking during the prototyping phase to get you ready for the actual build. Teams that have a strong process for prototyping usually come to competition more prepared with the knowledge of how certain systems work together on the field.

The Role of CAD

At this point, it may be helpful to take a look at the kinds of tools your team will have for the design process. CAD stands for computer-aided design software. It is important to note that the design is computer *aided* and not computer *performed*. This means that all the design work will still be the responsibility of the team, which must think about every last nut and bolt required to put a system together. That being said, CAD programs are incredibly powerful tools in that they act as a system of enhanced design workflow, documentation, and simulation. As students and members of robotics teams, you will all have access to free licenses of industry-standard CAD programs like Autodesk Inventor, Solidworks, and NX. To

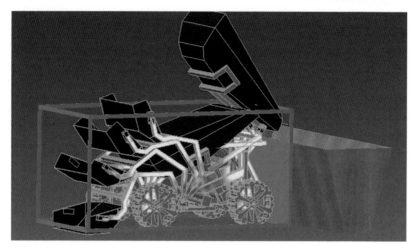

This is a CAD model of a moon-mining robot showing range of motion for a dumping sequence.

take advantage of these offers, simply look into what programs sponsor the robotics organization you're competing in and fill out student applications. Some licenses are awarded to teams and can be given out by mentors. Other licenses are free by just proving that you are a high school student using the software for educational purposes. This capability is really tremendous. In order to use these programs in the workforce, companies sometimes pay tens of thousands of dollars for the same software that you will get to use free of charge.

So what is a CAD program like and how can it benefit your design process? In a nutshell, software of this type provides an environment to draw objects in two or three dimensions. Any drawing you do on paper is going to be two dimensional, with a mere representation of depth. The advantage of working in three dimensions with CAD software is that you have the opportunity to manipulate a three-dimensional object from any angle by only "drawing" the object once. Where pencil and paper would have required three different drawings to capture the front, back, and top-down views of an object, CAD programs allow you to see any view from a single design.

Getting Started

Never drawn in three dimensions before? Don't worry: you'll always be starting with two dimensions and performing other actions to get the third. Say you want to start designing the robot's frame out of rectangular sections of aluminum stock. For a robust frame, you have decided to use 3-inch (7.6 cm) by 1-inch (2.5 cm) rectangular tubing. In CAD, you can begin this drawing by using the 3 × 1 dimension to make one face of the rectangular prism. Using this two-dimensional sketch, you can perform an "**extrusion.**" This will take the 3 × 1 face and create the last dimension based on how long you choose to make the extrusion. Thus, if you wanted a 3-foot (0.9-meter) section of rectangular stock for two of the walls of your robot frame, you could input 3 feet into the extrusion function in the program. As a matter of efficiency, you also now have the object complete, so you simply need to duplicate it to get the second 3-foot section.

Now that you have two pieces complete, you'll need to find a way to fit them into the three-dimensional build space of the design. This means that the duplicated object needs to be "constrained" to certain dimensions relative to the placement of the first object. If you know the robot needs to be 2.5 feet (0.75 m) long, you can constrain the outer faces of the two rectangular prisms at a distance of 2.5 feet. The two pieces will also have to be parallel in the other axis, though. To fix this, you can constrain the 3 × 1 faces of both pieces to each other.

This will make it so any time you move one of the objects in the frame, the rest of the frame will move with it, keeping the structure of the robot together.

CAD as Documentation

A CAD model can be powerful in its ability to go above and beyond the capabilities of a two-dimensional drawing. One of the most important aspects of this is the ability of a model to inform your team of design constraints and considerations between subsystems. Need to know if your arm will fit into the robot without obstructing the winch mechanism? Assuming all of the parts in your model have been accurately measured, you should be able to avoid running for a tape measure to figure out that question. A running CAD model can serve as a reference for the design of the entire robot. This means that CAD doesn't have to be your primary design tool in order to provide useful information for the team. In fact, many successful teams design and build systems before ever importing them into the computer. It is very good practice to have files backed up for the entire robot to make sure that there is room for all necessary systems and components.

The Efficiency of CAD

Another attractive feature of CAD is the fact that you can import files into your designs from other places. This means that you can download 3-D part files from the Internet and use them in your design process to get you there faster. In fact, if your robotics competition has a suggested or included kit of parts, chances are most of those parts have been put into CAD and are floating around the net for general use. This will really help kick-start your design process if you're looking for ideas or specific parts that may be difficult to get the dimensions of. The good news is many part manufacturers have made a point to include CAD models of parts on their data sheets and on their websites for download. Ordering an actuator from the Internet and need to make sure it fits your robot build? Simply download the CAD file and import it into your running model. This method can save you critical time spent measuring and figuring out how to attach new parts to the robot.

CAD and Simulation

Perhaps one of the most powerful and important aspects of CAD software is its ability to run physical simulations on your designs. Worried that your robot is in danger of tipping over in various positions? You can use CAD programs to calculate the center of gravity of the robot in every position, given that you have accurate documentation of the materials used on the system. CAD programs have comprehensive lists of material properties like the weight of aluminum or steel, the tensile strength of a material under load, or the heat tolerances of a piece of plastic. All of this can be incredibly useful when determining potential issues with your designs. A common example of this could be calculating whether the joint of a robotic arm is strong enough to handle the weight of a game component. Using the dimensions and properties of the game element, you can run **finite element analysis** on the joint to see if the weld is likely to break or not. This can even account for

PRINTING IN THREE DIMENSIONS

If your design team becomes proficient in CAD software, you can potentially make use of **3-D printers** for rapid prototyping and even some direct applications to the robot. Once you complete the design of a 3-D part, you can export it to a 3-D printer's slicing software. Every 3-D printer should come with its own software, or be compatible with commonly used programs. So why is it called "slicing software?" Slicing is a reference to the way in which 3-D printers have to break models down into individual layers or slices to create a three-dimensional object. Imagine if you were asked to make a solid cylinder out of pieces of paper. You would have to take the shape of a circle and make a stack of pieces tall enough to constitute your three dimensional cylinder. Most commercial 3-D printers operate on this same principle, by printing objects one layer at a time with thin lines of melted plastic material. The depth of a single layer might not look like much more than a two-dimensional piece of paper, but with all the layers added up, you can print an entire object.

3-D printers allow you to make small, potentially complex parts in a fraction of the time that it would take to machine the same piece. Especially useful for prototyping, 3-D printed pieces can help convey an idea or concept without having to spend a lot of time cutting, drilling, or shaping a material. The spools of plastic for printers are also very cheap relative to other materials used to make 3-D objects, so prototyping can be cheaper after the initial cost of the printer itself. Objects made by 3-D printers are most effective when used in smaller assemblies that don't take on large amounts of stress. They are also great for making last minute aesthetics to make the robot look like it's a member of your team!

A 3-D printed gear has been attached to a motor shaft. It is best not to rely on printed materials for critical gears.

While 3-D printing offers a fast, cheap solution for creating parts, the parts come with a few drawbacks. A 3-D printed piece is not made to withstand significant force, pressure, or heat. It's best not to rely on a 3-D printer for critical gears or robotic arm joints. ABS and PLA plastic are very brittle and can "delaminate" easily. Delamination is the point at which the printed layers exceed their adhesive capabilities and separate in the direction of the layers. This is even more likely to happen if the part is under any heated conditions. ABS and PLA are two commonly used plastics in 3-D printer extruders. They have relatively low melting points of 330 degrees Fahrenheit (165 degrees Celsius) and 390°F (200°C), respectively. However, they have what's called a **glass transition temperature**, which is the point at which it solidifies at around 158°F (70°C) to 194°F (90°C). This means that any temperature above that range will make the parts deform easily, so avoid local heat from friction or electronics.

expected vibrations from the motors on the arm or other related variables to replicate expected conditions of operation.

"But It Fit in CAD!"

We have talked up the immense benefits of using CAD software in robot design. It is also important to bring up its possible shortcomings and the reality of physically building the robot. In the computer, you are free to design components with any dimensions and tolerances. In reality, you will find that machining parts never quite achieves the level of precision that you'd get from computer simulation. Especially if you're drilling holes or cutting pieces by hand, you should always be designing parts knowing an acceptable margin for error. For instance, a 0.25-inch (0.6 cm) motor shaft will not fit in a 0.25-inch hole the way your CAD design might suggest. The hole will need to be oversized by a couple thousandths of an inch in order to provide a so-called **slip fit**. A slip fit allows the dowel or motor shaft to slip in and out of the holes easily. There are lots of useful charts and tables out there to show you recommended drill bits for common screw sizes, and other machining-related problems. In short, don't assume that manufacturing a part will always be as easy as typing in the dimensions on a computer. Real materials have impurities and properties that cause them to react in certain ways to being cut, heated, or bent. It is very important to understand the materials you're working with in order to effectively enact your designs.

Be thorough in your designs and measurements to be sure that what you are putting into the computer can actually be built. It is very common for teams designing exclusively in the computer to forget that design includes both mechanical and electrical components. In other words, it's easy to forget that you need space to run wires to all your components! There's nothing worse than building up an entire system only to find that it doesn't have enough room for actually connecting motors or controllers to the power module. To circumvent this, some teams even model their wiring down to the last crimp and zip tie to prevent design issues and give comprehensive documentation of their robot in case anything happens.

Conclusion

Your team should now have at least an outline to work from in terms of designing a competition robot. As stated before, there is lots of supplementary research out there on all of the mechanisms mentioned in this chapter. Every design can be refined through further understanding of the physical principles that apply to a given system. Use this chapter as a jumping off point to figure out what ensemble of mechanisms will help your team succeed this season.

We have thus far talked about a few possible systems and strategies involved in robot design. In the next chapter, we'll get down to the real nuts and bolts of figuring out how to make a working system. Every moving part needs **power**. How much power does it need? What balance can be attained between power and control? What do these power requirements mean in terms of the kinds of components that need to be on the robot? Keep these questions in mind as we make the next steps toward instantiating, or turning into reality, your robot designs.

This robot needed to lift large game variables high off the ground to stack them and score points at competition.

3 Electrical and Mechanical Power

At this point, your team should already have some solid ideas that have been prototyped and tested. You may have already gotten some good indicators as to the kinds of motors, actuators, and servos to use from this process. Now it's time to identify exactly what your robot will need to consistently tackle game challenges. From your tests, you should have a range of results from both successful and (especially) unsuccessful trials. Use this data as a jumping off point to set the team in the right direction. For instance, if your shooting mechanism failed to reach its targets in terms of distance, you can assess the need for a faster motor, a spinning wheel of larger diameter, or more or less friction against the other wheel or plane. These are a few examples of the ways in which your team will need to investigate requirements for power and force.

When looking at your options for various motors, you may have noticed a number of specifications for expected or theoretical performance. Some of these specs could be "no load RPMs," "free current," "stall current," "maximum power," and "stall torque." In this chapter, we'll break down what all these terms mean and how they apply to the overall picture of the robot. There's an exact correlation between the mechanical capabilities of a motor and the electrical requirements to run that motor. As a result, we'll be going over some basic calculations for electricity in order to discuss the physical capabilities of mechanisms.

The Physics of Power

This chapter goes over the basics of power for motors and mechanisms on the robot. In order to talk about power, we're going to need a quick primer on electricity. In most cases, your robot will be powered via an onboard rechargeable battery. This battery will generally have a high maximum current to handle all the motors and controllers on board the robot. Up to this point, your team may be familiar with physics and the some of the basic theory behind electricity, but here is your first chance to see the power that those formulas bring to the table. Let's begin to apply some of that hard-earned knowledge from the classroom.

If you've already gotten through a physics class, chances are you already know Ohm's law by heart. Even if you do, though, you may not have gotten a chance to see how it applies to your personal experiences. So what can $V = IR$ do for you? Let's first break down its constituent parts. The V stands for **voltage**. I in Ohm's law represents current in amperes, or "amps," which is the rate of electrical flow in a circuit. The R stands for **resistance** and is measured in "ohms." Voltage is the potential energy between a positive and negative terminal of a circuit. If you imagine electricity kind of like water flowing from a large tank into a hose (high potential energy to low,) then voltage would represent the pressure of the water in the system. In this analogy, a wire would be like a hose that comes from the source (positive terminal of a battery) of the tank. Current in this case is the rate at which water flows through the system out of the hose. An ampere is actually a measurement of electrons transferred per second through a circuit. Resistance, then, would be the size of the hose. If the hose diameter becomes smaller, the amount of current flowing through it reduces. Think if you had two tanks the same size but with different

The water pressure increases when the mouth of the hose is limited by physical resistance.

diameter hoses. The one with the larger diameter hose will have a much stronger flow if the tanks are filled with the same amount of water, thus having the same pressure or "voltage." As resistance goes up (smaller hose), the voltage stays the same but the current drops proportionally.

Now let's talk power. Power is a measurement of *energy* from an electrical circuit over time. A watt is the measurement of power that is the transfer of energy at 1 joule per second. In the formula $P = VI$, you can see how power is simply the amount of potential energy (voltage) multiplied by the rate of electron flow (current) in a system. Stepping back to our water tank analogy, power would be like the amount of force you have to move a wheel in a water mill. If you get a larger tank than you had before (higher pressure) but keep the same current flow, you'll be able to move the wheel with greater force. Power in a general sense is *work over time*. So in this case, we're assessing the work being done by an electric circuit, meaning its ability to provide power to components on the robot.

Unit Conversion and the Right Motor

Now that we've discussed a bit of the basics behind power, we can head into the process of selecting a good motor for your application. DC motors usually come within a kit of parts for a robot team. These motors can absolutely be sufficient for some mechanisms, but don't feel as though you are being forced to design around them. Other motors are commercially available and sometimes cheap for specific applications. Be sure to check out the helpful links and resources section at the end of the book for places to get good robot motors and accessories. When going through this process, though, it's important to know exactly what you want from a motor before spending valuable resources on it.

You should be able to identify the task you're trying to perform, the control you want to have, and the amount of time you want to do it in. These three aspects will ultimately determine the calculations your team will use to see if a motor is right for a given application. Those three things, however, are not immediately obvious from looking at the specifications of a motor. On a product information page, you are likely to see things like power, torque, and speed listed instead. In order to address the problem at hand, your team will have to do some unit conversion to get the information you need.

Let's start with an example application. Say your robot has an arm that is going to be lifting a game piece that weighs 10 pounds (4.5 kilograms). In order to successfully score that game piece, the robot has to lift it at least 3 feet (0.9 meters) in the air. Given that a competition round is fast and there could be many game pieces to score, your team decides that it needs to be able to lift a single piece in four seconds or less to be competitive. While this list might seem like a very basic set of requirements, it actually gives us enough information to crunch the numbers for a new motor.

Looking around on the web, you see that the power of a motor is listed in watts. Watts are a measurement of electrical power over time. A single watt, for instance, is the power usage of 1 joule per second. Joules are a force measurement.

This is the first unit we'll be converting to see if your robot can lift game pieces. The information page may also list the horsepower of the motor. However, given that DC motors are often a fraction of one horsepower, it's common for this to be unlisted. Horsepower is a measurement of force, distance, and time, making it very valuable to our calculations. A single horsepower can be converted into 745.7 watts, meaning we can take the wattage of the motor and set up a proportion. For instance, a 300-watt motor would be equal to approximately 0.4 horsepower.

One horsepower actually measures 550 **foot-pounds** per second. This is significant because we have in our list both a measurement of pounds (10-pound game piece) as well as a distance in feet (>3 feet of lift). We can set up our problem by multiplying 10 pounds × 3 feet. Then, we take that value and divide by the amount of time we want to lift the game piece. So with a time of four seconds, we can calculate a desired value of 7.5 foot-pounds per second. We have now converted to the same unit as horsepower, so let's express our value as such: 7.5/550 = 0.0136 horsepower. Now that we have a desired horsepower, we can easily convert back into watts to find a minimum power value to achieve our goal. A horsepower of 0.0136 comes out to 10.1415 watts, meaning that a 15-watt motor should give your team more than enough wiggle room to get the job done.

These calculations can be very valuable for a number of applications. While lifting an object over a set amount of time may have a rather direct correlation to horsepower, you can use methods to tackle problems like drive speed. Let's say your team wants to play heavy defense this year, meaning you need a strong drivetrain with the ability to push opponents out of the way if necessary. The thing that makes this problem significantly different is the element of friction with the wheels contacting the floor. However, having an ideal horsepower in mind can be a good place to start for being able to drive without fear. Simply set up the problem with a few expected values like the speed and weight of your robot. Next, add in the hypothetical weight of an opposing robot and calculate how much horsepower it would take to easily move the combined load. While the opposing robot could be driving head-on into you or simply stationary, you should be able to crunch the numbers with this method to get you a ballpark figure of how powerful your drive motors need to be to play your strategy.

Pulse Width Modulation and Your Motors

When considering the power requirements for running various motors, it may be helpful to go into a bit more depth on how that power is actually getting to the motors. Motors now are controlled by electronic speed controllers, or ESCs. They act as an intermediate device between a **microcontroller**, the power source, and a motor. So how exactly does a controller like this regulate the speed of the motor? Years ago, analog speed controllers simply regulated the voltage from a power source that would determine how fast the motor goes; in the digital age, ESCs handles things a bit differently. For instance, an analog speed controller might output 6VDC to a 12VDC motor to run it at something like half speed (motor efficiency is never quite this linear, though). An ESC, on the other hand, only supplies the motor with the maximum 12VDC and still manages to run the motor at different speeds.

In order to achieve variable speed with a given voltage, an ESC has to run a series of on and off pulses. This means that the motor can *only* be supplied with 12 volts or 0 volts and oscillates between them at a very rapid pace. The narrower the pulse of 12 volts, the slower the motor will go. The wider the pulse, the more time you'll be supplying the motor with its maximum voltage, increasing its speed. The period of time between pulses is referred to as a **duty cycle**. In a simplified way, you can think of this literally as the percentage of the time that a motor is performing its duty of spinning at 12VDC.

A given duty cycle can produce a specific speed because it produces an average voltage over time. This is to say that you could take the number of pulses in a second, or the frequency, and calculate the percentage of that second that the motor was on or off. For instance, if the 12-volt pulse is only on for 25 percent of the time, or 0.25 seconds, you can represent that as a proportion of the maximum voltage. The average voltage over that single second would be 3VDC for that pulse frequency. This method of control is called **pulse width modulation** because of the relationship between the width of the "on" state and the average voltage output to a device.

Pneumatic Systems and Compressors

Pneumatic systems use compressed air to move robotic mechanisms. In order to have compressed air on board the robot, you will need either a **compressor** with an air tank or a pre-pressurized air tank. A compressor is a device that converts electrical energy into stored potential energy of a pressurized gas. This means that you will use your robot's battery to power

This pneumatic control system with a compressor, solenoids, and air hoses is used to power an actuator on the top of the robot.

a small compressor in order to generate enough pressure to operate a given pneumatic system. You usually want to invest in an onboard compressor if the need for pressurized air exceeds the capacity of a tank that is sized reasonably for the robot. Additionally, robotics competitions usually limit the size of an onboard pressurized air tank as a matter of safety. Be sure to read up on the technical requirements of pneumatic systems in the game rules before constructing a high-pressured monstrosity of a robot.

Pneumatic systems come with a set of advantages and disadvantages that may depend on your application. Using compressed air can be more reliable, accurate, and consistent than electrical components due to the natural energy inefficiency of electrical components. Pneumatic actuators tend to be more sturdy and reliable than a system of similar function like a rack and pinion. Pneumatic components have a very long operating life and need little maintenance, which is why they are frequently selected for industrial robotics applications.

Compressed air is measured in **PSI**, or pounds per square inch. This is a measurement of potential stored energy and represents the amount of pressure in a given volume. Air tanks for small robots usually have a maximum pressure of around 120 PSI. While the size of such a tank might not be very large, it still carries enormous mechanical potential for robotic applications.

In order to control compressed air systems, you need valves that open and close rapidly to allow for exact PSI tolerances. While it is possible to use simple mechanical valves, it's not likely to produce a consistent or desirable result. Instead, you can use electrically triggered valves known as **solenoids**. This means that you will be able to control large pneumatic systems remotely from your robot's microprocessor. In other words, the solenoid does the mechanical opening and closing very quickly

CHEAT SHEET

So, how many PSI will you need to release to fully extend an actuator? How big of a tank will you need to sustain pressure long enough to lift an object overhead? If the tank runs out, how big or fast of a compressor will you need to regain sufficient PSI for operation? All of these questions can be answered with a number of pneumatics calculations. The most straightforward way to address these concerns is by referencing a pneumatic calculation chart. These charts are used widely by machinists and engineers to look at the force and time requirements of their application. Here you can see the linear relationship between the diameter of a pneumatic cylinder and its output force based on the pressure in the cylinder.

AIR LINE PRESSURE (PSI)

BORE SIZE	80	85	90	95	100	105	110	115	120
1½	141	150	159	168	177	186	194	203	212
2	251	267	283	298	314	330	346	361	377
2½	393	417	442	466	491	515	540	565	589
3¼	664	705	747	788	830	871	913	954	995
4	1005	1068	1131	1194	1257	1319	1382	1445	1508
5	1571	1669	1767	1865	1964	2062	2160	2258	2356
6	2262	2403	2545	2686	2827	2969	3110	3252	3393

NOTE: "Push" Forces in pounds = (Cylinder Bore Diameter)^2 x 0.7854 x Line Pressure

This chart shows the bore size in inches of a pneumatic cylinder relative to its output force. It can help you pick a cylinder size for a pneumatic application.

PNEUMATICS AND ANIMATRONIC ROBOTS

Pneumatic systems excel at a number of industrial applications because of their reliability and relatively low need of maintenance. One particular industry that takes advantage of these characteristics is animatronics. Ever been to a theme park and seen mechanical characters performing the same repeated motions with precision and fluidity? Animatronic robots use pneumatic actuators for every movement you can imagine. Whether it's a pirate raising an arm or a raptor lashing out at an audience, pneumatic systems drive

An animatronic dinosaur is controlled by many large pneumatic actuators on the inside, as well as many smaller ones for eye and skin movements.

the movement of theme park robots. These mechanisms provide the most efficient solution for being able to repeat performances hundreds of times a day for theme park goers.

The size of the actuator or compressed air motor depends on the application. Even for small, delicate movements like facial expressions, tiny actuators are used to move the "skeletal" structures underneath the robot's skin. Animatronics companies use very special silicon composites for their skins to give skeletal movements more realism and character. In order to capture such realistic expressions and movements, a facial system can have dozens of pneumatic actuators controlling multiple subsystems. Try to think of the number of movements you can make with just your mouth. These engineers figure out ways to represent as many of those movements as possible by precisely orchestrating the firing of tiny solenoids to get different movement patterns. Even the eyes of an animatronic robot are controlled by actuators. In order to achieve this, the ends of the actuators are connected to swiveling joints that allow for circular movements of the robot's eyes.

multi-stage, cylinders can extend to lengths based on the size and number of nested cylindrical sections. These systems can be great for reaching tall goals without the need for gears or motors and generally fit a smaller profile than other more robust mechanisms.

Wiring, Crimps, and Fuses

When you're wiring the robot, there are a few important things to keep in mind to ensure safe and stable operation. It may be somewhat obvious to think that electrical components with higher power needs will require a larger wire or cable to operate. Likewise, small digital devices can have wires that are only a few strands thick. The reason for this is that wires, just like any electrical device, have a current capacity. In our previous discussion of Ohm's law, we went over the relationship between power, current, voltage, and resistance. In order to describe those principles, we used the example of a garden hose with flowing water. Imagine for a second a scenario in which the flow running through the hose exceeds the pressure rating of the hose itself. That is kind of like the current capacity of a wire. If electrons are flowing at a rate that exceeds the physical capabilities of the strands of wire, it will generate massive amounts of heat. In fact, significantly overshooting a wire's current rating can result in a wire catching fire, incinerating the insulation material and creating an exposed conductor which can wreak havoc on surrounding systems. As fun as that may be to watch, we want to avoid setting fire to our robots at all costs. In this section, we'll go over ways to create electrically safe connections, keeping power and current requirements in mind as we go along.

We talked earlier about Ohm's law and the relationship between voltage, current, and power. This relationship is yet again integral to making decisions about how to properly and safely put the robot together. The robot's onboard battery is the source of power for every component on board. Even if there are pneumatic systems, the potential energy created by the compressors needs the battery to function. As a result, it's good to identify the power consumption of all of the systems on the robot.

While your team isn't likely to eat through a battery's entire charge in a single round, there are other significant considerations to be aware of. For instance, the power consumption of a motor will determine the size of the wire you use to power it. Wires have a "peak current" rating, meaning that there is a maximum number of amps that can flow through them. If you know the voltage that your battery is outputting and the wattage of your motor, you can determine how much current will be flowing through the wire. Let's say a motor is max 300 watts and your battery supplies 24VDC. If $P = VI$, then what would be the **amperage** running through the wire? You could modify the equation into $I = P/V$ or $I = 300$ watts/24 volts. This comes out to a total of 12.5 amps, which is a decent amount of current for a small wire to handle.

Wires are measured on the **AWG**, or American Wire Gauge, scale. Effectively, the cross section of a wire, meaning its diameter and number of strands, determines the gauge. The larger the diameter, the greater amount of current can safely flow through it. AWG is scaled inversely, meaning that as the wire gauge goes up, the diameter goes down.

Another relevant factor is length of the wire. Electrical resistance is a physical property defined by collisions of electrons with atoms of the conductor material. Since a longer wire will have a greater number of atoms for the electrons to collide with over a given distance, the resistance increases relative to the wire's length. Additionally, the smaller the wire gauge, the greater the resistance will be over a distance due to the increased ratio of atoms to conductivity. Luckily, robotics applications usually call for wire lengths of less than 10 feet (3 m), making the added resistance of the wire negligible to most power calculations. For a 22-gauge wire, you would have to have a section of more than 60 feet (18 m) to produce a single ohm of resistance. For our application, 14 AWG wire should be sufficient for the theoretical maximum of 12.5 amps drawn by the motor. In fact, most motors come with wires already connected, so it's good practice to match the gauge provided by the manufacturer as well.

A Dead Short

Let's talk some more about disaster scenarios. Imagine for a second that your robot is competing and somehow becomes entangled on an opponent's robot. As the bedlam ensues, one of your unsecured wires catches on a sprocket or sharp corner of a mechanism. Your robot is now rolling around with exposed wires both red and black that used to be connected to a motor. The connection came directly from the batteries, so the leads are a hot 24VDC ready to arc at any moment. If for some reason something like this were to occur, it could start a fire, or fry other major components on board the robot. How can we avoid such a calamity?

The answer (in addition to diligent cable management) is **fuses**. Fuses are electrical devices that are made specifically to sacrifice themselves by taking the force of shorts and electrical spikes. You might have heard the term "blowing a fuse," referring to a very angry situation. Likewise, blowing an actual fuse means that a circuit's current capacity (determined by the value of the fuse) has been exceeded. A **dead short** is a direct, unmitigated connection between positive and negative terminals in an electric circuit. This means that the maximum possible current flow of a source will be wreaking havoc on whatever it touches. In the case of a battery, this can mean fires or explosions.

Having fuses is a good line of defense for unforeseen shorts because it allows you to simply replace a blown fuse instead of an expensive device like a microcontroller. Most robotics kits have power distribution boards with built-in fuse holders. Be sure to identify the expected current draw of every fused component and select a value that suits the needs of your robot. This keeps not only your robot but the whole team safe from electrical mishaps.

Solid Electrical Connections

In order to ensure that good clean power is provided to all your components, you'll need to make connections with quality soldering or crimping. Loose connections can be just as dangerous as exposed wires when it comes to potential shorts if not properly insulated. This section will go over good wiring practices and techniques to follow when putting the robot together. There are many ways to make good electrical connections, so don't think that expensive tools and connectors are the only way to have a stable circuit.

Let's start by going over a few basic kinds of electrical connectors. These connectors are all widely available on the Internet and can be a great way to increase the security of a circuit. First up are **Anderson Power Poles**. These connectors are kind of like the LEGOs of the electrical world as they snap together and come in a few different sizes and colors for various applications. The crimping tool required is fairly cheap and extremely easy to use. These connectors, however, are sized for wire size 22 AWG and larger, so smaller wires for digital communications will need different solutions.

Next we have **ring terminals** and fork terminals. These are crimped to wires that need to be connected to lugs that screw into place. It is common for robot power distribution modules to have connecting lugs like this.

On a similar note, screw terminals also secure wires with pressure applied from a screw. This kind of terminal can use bare wire, however, if the terminal is tightened properly and a threadlocker has been applied to prevent back-outs. This is the least reliable connection on this list and sometimes requires a dab of silicon compound to keep wires snugly in place. Alternatively, you can use **ferrule crimps** to consolidate wire strands for screw terminals and reduce the risk of broken wires.

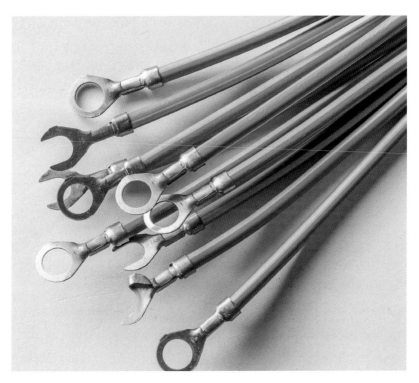

Ring terminals and fork terminals crimped to the ends of wires make connecting to lugs easier to do.

Blade connectors or **quick connects** can be a good insulated solution for connections between wires. Many circuit breakers and fuses also have this kind of terminal.

For higher amperage applications, you can use bullet connectors, which are popular among RC vehicle enthusiasts. These can be effective for making motors easily detachable while retaining a connection with high current draw.

Heat Shrink, Twisting, and Shielding

Heat shrink is a material that does exactly what its name suggests: shrinks when heat is applied. This stuff is absolutely necessary to clean wiring as it can cover up soldered joints or exposed parts of connectors. Heat shrink is kind of like wire insulation you can put on after the fact, making it incredibly valuable for repairs and modifications as well. Heat shrink does necessitate a bit of forethought and process, however. Make sure to slide the heat shrink over a wire before crimping a large connection. That way you can still shrink the material down small enough to hold the wires.

Solder sleeves are a wonderful invention as they take the technical work out of soldering.

They contain a ring of solder inside a sleeve of heat shrink that contracts when heated and binds to wire insulation. The solder has a lower melting temperature than the wires you are connecting. Slide the solder sleeve over a wire and then twist together the exposed wires you want to connect. (Solder sleeves may come with a terminal attached; you slide the wire inside the terminal before applying heat.) Then, center the sleeve over the exposed wires. Using only a high temperature heat gun, you simply focus heat on the solder joint ring inside the heat shrink until the flux that comes on the solder ring gets hot enough to flow through the wires. Flux is a material that cleans the heated surfaces, preventing corrosion and enhancing the soldering bond. These can be very handy, especially when working with small wires or creating a junction of multiple wires.

Without the solder sleeve, you must apply your own flux, heat it so it flows through the wires, heat solder so it covers the wires, then use a tube of heat shrink pulled over the joint to seal it.

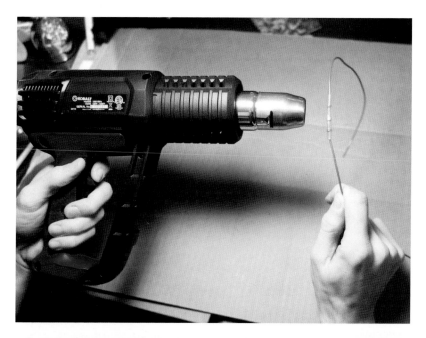

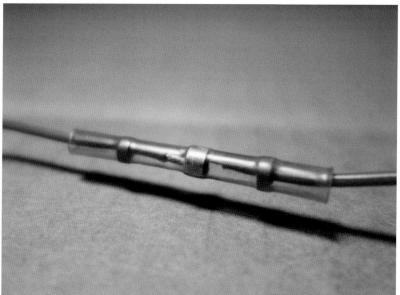

A student uses a heat gun to connect two wires in a solder sleeve (above). *A ring of solder is inside the sleeve* (below).

If wires are ever in contact with moving parts, it is wise to invest in shielding that is more heavy duty than the wire insulation. Friction can wear down or even eat away at insulation over time, which could lead to shorts or broken connections. Bundles of wires can be put in braided shielding to increase resilience and minimize the ability for interference. If you suspect there is electromagnetic interference in communications cables like Ethernet, you can also use special shielding to filter out various high or low oscillating

ATTACHING TIPS

Your wiring can get cleaned up significantly by twisting together pairs or related bundles. Individual wires have a tendency to get caught up in everything or entangle themselves. The more wires are twisted together, the less likely they are to get bunched up and the easier they are to work with when routing them through frame components. Once the wires are bundled, zip ties make quick work of securing bundles to various parts of the robot, making for safe wires that are out of the way of moving parts.

frequencies. You may have seen a small black ring around one of your USB cables. This is a ferrite toroid used to filter electromagnetic frequencies much the same way and could be used to protect communications signals on the robot if interference is suspected.

Conclusion

In this chapter, we explored a wide range of topics related to power, electricity, and connections on the robot. Hopefully this section serves as a good buffer for the next chapter, which focuses on getting down and building the robot. With the knowledge of safe, effective electrical practices, your team should be able to confidently take the next steps toward a fully realized set of concepts and mechanisms. Armed with an understanding of which components to use, the fabrication and construction steps should be an exploration of creative methods to make it all come together.

Students must wear proper eye protection when using equipment, such as a drill press, to fabricate parts.

4 Putting It All Together

At this point, your team has designed a number of mechanisms of which you've made prototypes to get proof of your designs. While some prototypes may still need further experimentation or tweaking, you should have a solid foundation to get started putting this robot together. In this chapter, we'll go over a number of construction approaches aimed both at teams with full machine shops as well as those that build out of their physics classroom. Even if your team is on a tight budget or doesn't have immediate access to machine equipment, we'll go over how creativity and strategic outreach can go a long way in the build season.

No matter what the starting resources of a team might be, creative solutions to design problems will make a winning robot. Even at the international stage of robotics competitions, teams using low-cost materials in effective ways can stand (and often *win*) against robots built under the guidance of multi-billion-dollar engineering companies. Don't be intimidated by the clean-cut look of veteran robot teams that have robot frames constructed from CNC waterjet parts with fancy lights and sounds. It's all still a design effort that has to be executed effectively in order to succeed.

Starting with the Basics

Let's say you're a rookie team with only a couple of hand tools and a kit of parts to your name. Where is a good place to jump in? The kits provided by your robotics program will usually have some powerful stuff in them. Even if in a first glance at the kit you don't see anything promising for use as a potential claw assembly or shooting mechanism, there are elements that can be used to immediate effect. There should at least be some frame components, wheels, and motors along with some sort of gearing system. If the length of these pieces doesn't fit the frame you had in mind, don't be afraid to start modifying them with the tools you have. A hand hacksaw can make quick work of hollow aluminum tubing. The kit of parts is only as useful as you can make it. This means that any modification is fair game for raw materials to get you closer to a robot frame.

Once you have frame pieces to your desired dimensions, you should be able to bolt the frame together with the hole patterns in the aluminum. If your frame components are without pre-existing holes, don't be afraid to drill right into the material.

During frame construction, your team should bear in mind ways to mount drive motors and gear assemblies for the wheels. You will almost always want a gear reduction on your drive motor to increase handling capabilities and make the robot drive more smoothly. This could be from a transmission box–style gear reduction or chain and sprocket. It will be up to your team to decide what balance of speed, torque, and control needs to be attained for your game challenges. Remember that even the frame and the drivetrain are design considerations and should be approached deliberately. A rectangular robot with four wheels isn't always the most ideal choice for a game. Moreover, modifications can be made to simple ideas, such as adding a suspension or an unconventional steering system.

RUN A TIGHT SHIP

It is critical to have the frame bolted tightly together with some kind of locking nut or threadlocker. Nuts with nylon inserts or threading adhesive like "Loctite" prevent the bolt from backing out and coming loose under the stress and vibrations of the robot. A tight, robust frame is the foundation of any good robot.

With the drivetrain secured firmly in the frame, you should be ready to move to the primary structures on the robot. This may be the point at which the kit of parts fails to reveal potential mechanisms to your team. Perhaps you can make a version of your design with the kit of parts, but in order to fully realize the idea, you'll need to look elsewhere for materials. Depending on the mechanism, it's not at all unusual to implement low-cost materials like wood, PVC, or scrap metal. If the team's budget is especially tight, many raw materials can be acquired through salvage or donation. Be sure to ask around local shops to see what's being unused or thrown out.

Sponsorship and Community Resources

While this chapter is focused on physically building the robot, a big part of this process may be getting involved with local industry firms or manufacturing outfits. The truth is, engineering and manufacturing companies know the value of teaching students like you hands-on skills. A robotics club, in a lot of ways, embodies the values of successful teaching and engineering companies. Your job as a team is to clearly explain your mission, your needs, and your appreciation of local involvement for the robotics season.

Reaching out to local industry professionals is often incredibly helpful for the support they can provide. Whether the help is monetary, dedicated shop time, or expert volunteer mentorship, the engineering community around you is an invaluable resource to your team. Let's go over some of the

Community and industry sponsors can be displayed proudly on plexiglass on the side of a robot.

ways to effectively approach local professionals as well as some of the reasons your team might reach out for assistance.

If your team lacks proper machine tools or manufacturing equipment, you can approach local firms for use of their machines and expertise. Always have a working prototype, CAD model, or thorough design drawings of the pieces you hope to make with them. This can be very helpful when you have a part in mind with no idea how it might actually be manufactured. This step is a great opportunity to get feedback on the actual process of machining parts. This will often involve revisiting and fine-tuning designs to accommodate the machining process. Try to think of the number of different operations it will take a machinist to perform if moving one or two axes at a time. With the exception of some very expensive computer numerically controlled (CNC) machines, most mills, **lathes,** and routers are limited to two or three axes of operation. This means that if you want holes drilled in both the top and side of an object, you'll need to reposition and re-center the piece before both can be achieved.

Even if a company doesn't have the time or staff to accommodate your build season, you can still reach out for financial support. This is typically most effective when the relationship has been secured before build season starts. However, it is very common to make requests for raw materials like steel, aluminum, plastic, or composites. In return, your team will get branding materials and proudly display your sponsors on the robot and any promotional team materials. High-caliber robot teams are often covered in a variety of branding from sponsors in their community, and it's easy to see why that's the case. Teams that are well connected and have reached out for help receive profound assistance from industry mentors and professionals.

Matching Methods

We have just gone over the role of community involvement and potential services offered by engineers. It is important, now, to look at some of the specific methods that you might look into for manufacturing parts on your robot. Most of these ways will require the use of professional machine equipment. As such, this section should help your team narrow down the types of local industry that you want to build relationships with. Do you require the assistance of welding, tube bending, or waterjet cutting? Will your parts need to have precision of 0.001 inches (0.02 millimeters)? The questions are a good starting place for figuring out which services your team will need to enact your more complicated designs.

Milling Machines

Mills are precision machines that use a high-RPM spindle to perform cutting operations. The piece(s) being manufactured are secured to a "table" which can shift precisely in three axes known as x, y, and z. The rotary cutting tool removes material as the table moves or "feeds" along one or more of the axes. This makes **milling machines** particularly adept at machining surfaces to a flat finish known as "facing." Additionally, milling machines are commonly used to put precision hole patterns or channels into pieces.

Mills are also commonly CNC. These CNC mills excel at all the aforementioned tasks and do so very efficiently. With a computer controlling the table movements and consequent tool pathing, you can ensure precision spacing between holes or channels in a piece. Perhaps even more importantly, CNC mills are not limited by the capabilities of a manual machine operator. This means that the computer can move the table in all three axes (x, y, and z) at once, allowing for the manufacturing of three dimensional curves. CNC milling machines can have five or even seven axes to work with, meaning that three dimensional shapes can be machined by reducing the number of times the part is positioned and jigged.

Lathes

Lathes perform a kind of inverse operation from a milling machine. Instead of securing a piece and rotating a cutting bit, a lathe spins *the piece itself* at high RPM and uses a fixed cutting bit to remove material. Lathes are used primarily for machining cylinders or circular objects. Manually operated lathes are great for making fittings for precision shafts or machining a flat face on a concentric piece. Any cuts that are made on a lathe are made symmetrically due to the high-speed rotation of the piece. At low speeds, however, a lathe can perform operations like cutting threads into the inside or outside of a tube or shaft.

CNC lathes, like their milling machine counterparts, have the advantage of being able to operate in multiple axes at once.

FEEDS AND SPEEDS

When working on machine equipment, how will you know which bit to choose? How do you know what speed to run the cutting bit or piece? How fast or slow should the feed rate be to ensure a clean cut without the possibility of breaking a cutting tool? The answer to all these questions is "Feeds and Speeds." For every possible material and operation, machinists and engineers over the years have compiled lists of appropriate tooling and operating parameters for successful machining. For instance, not all cutting bits are created equal. Some have only a single cutting element called a "flute." Single flute bits are good at cutting plastics without generating excess heat that might melt the material in the cutting process.

Cutting aluminum requires cutting bits with far more flutes to remove material more consecutively through the feed. There is a corresponding feed and speed for just about any operation down to how many thousandths of an inch you want to remove with each pass. The smaller the cut, the faster you can move. Larger cuts or harder materials like steel require slow speeds and ample lubrication for good, safe cuts. Check out this example of a "feeds and speeds" chart for basic aluminum machining on a mill.

NAME	SB#	ONSRUD SERIES	CUT	CHIP LOAD PER LEADING EDGE	FLUTES	FEED RATE (IPS)	FEED RATE (IPM)	RPM	MAX CUT
1" 60° Carbide V cutter	13648	37 - 82	1 x D	.004-.006	2	2.4 - 3.6		18,000	
¼" Straight V Carbide Tipped End Mill	13642	48 - 005	1 x D	.005-.007	1	1.5 - 2.1	90-126	18,000	
½" Straight V Carbide Tipped End Mill	13564	48 - 072	1 x D	.006-.008	2	3.6 - 4.8		18,000	
¼" Upcut Carbide End Mill	13528	52 - 910	1 x D	.006-.008	2	3.6 - 4.8		18,000	
¼" Downcut Carbide End Mill	13507	57 - 910	1 x D	.005-.007	2	3.0 - 4.2		18,000	
¼" Upcut Carbide End Mill	1108	65 - 025	1 x D	.004-.006	1	1.2 - 1.8		18,000	
⅛" Tapered Carbide Upcut Ball End Mill	13636	77 - 102	1 x D	.003-.005	2	1.8 - 3.0		18,000	
1-¼" Carbide Tipped Surfacing Cutter	12555	91 - 000	½-¾ x D		2		200-600	12,000 - 16,000	⅛"

This example chart is for cutting hard wood material on a small CNC router.

This makes a CNC lathe capable of machining spheres or elliptical pieces. This technique can be great for making ball joints for mechanisms to be able to move in multiple axes.

Routers

Routers are very similar to milling machines but keep the piece fixed in a single location and move the spindle. As a result, routers are less apt to take on large cutting bits as the spindle has to be small enough to move around on a "gantry" system. Much like a prize-grabbing machine moves the claw around on two sets of rails known as a gantry, routers use the same system to move the head of a cutting tool. Routers are not quite as robust as mills are, however, and are limited in many cases to cutting softer materials like wood, plastic, and sometimes aluminum. CNC routers are perhaps the most accessible machines in terms of price for a robotics team. They are great for rapid prototyping and even making some aluminum components for the robot. In some cases, you are limited only by the maximum bed size of the routing table.

Welding and Plasma Cutting

Welding is defined as a joining process of two metals (or thermoplastics) using fusion to melt the base materials together in conjunction with an added filler metal. This means that both pieces are superheated until the metal transitions into a liquid state, flowing together in a puddle of molten material. There are a number of different methods for superheating the material using both electrical and chemical means. Let's introduce a few of the kinds of welding commonly used on robots.

Gas tungsten arc welding, known more commonly as TIG (tungsten inert gas) welding, uses a tungsten electrode to transfer current to the metal. This method requires a shielding gas like argon in the "torch," which prevents contaminants (like oxygen) from entering the weld. Oxygen can combine with carbon dioxide to form pores in the weld, making it weaker, and it can also lead to corrosion. TIG welders wield the torch in their primary hand and feed the filler material or rod into the puddle with their other hand. This takes a decent amount of dexterity and a steady hand to produce quality welds with good penetration (distance fusion extends in the base metal).

Gas metal arc welding, or MIG (metal insert gas), is perhaps the most common form of welding. Similar to TIG welding, MIG uses a gas shield (usually argon based) to protect the weld. The primary difference is that MIG welders use an automatically feeding wire gun to lay down filler material. This wire gun performs both the fusion and the infill by making electrical contact with the wire that spools out. MIG welding can be used for both steel and aluminum and is a bit more like operating a hot glue gun in terms of dexterity.

Shielded metal arc welding, or "stick welding," uses a consumable electrode with a catalyst called "flux" in it. The electrode is secured in a holder and slowly melts away over the course of the weld. The flux protects the puddle of the weld similarly to the gas shield. The flux cools into slag, which is a byproduct of the stick welding process. Stick welding is perhaps the most modest of the electrical methods in terms of required

Stick welding requires little equipment, but anyone trying it will need proper clothing and a face mask.

equipment. With only a power supply, holder, and consumable electrodes, your team could be stick welding the robot frame together in no time.

An oxyacetylene torch is another popular form of welding. This process is very different as it uses the pressure of two combined gases (oxygen and acetylene) to create a high-intensity flame. By varying the ratio of oxygen to acetylene, you can increase or decrease the heat of the flame on the regulating nozzle. This method can be more time consuming on thick materials because of the direct heat transfer from the torch to the material. Similar in practice to TIG welding, the operator holds the torch to the materials until they flow together, then adds rod with the other hand. This is definitely the most "old school" method but can be very successful if done correctly. Oxyacetylene torch setups are very cheap relative to other welding methods and can be a great place to start for teams on a budget in need of welding supplies.

Plasma cutting is a related practice and is often available at shops with welding operations. The plasma is an ionized gas. Plasma cutting is similar insofar as it uses an electrode to create an arc to a conductive material like steel, aluminum, or brass. This method uses compressed gas like oxygen to create a plasma jet straight through the material. Plasma cutters can move at high speeds and make precision cuts, making them great for both hand and CNC operation.

Sheet Metal and Bending Operations

Sometimes your designs or assemblies will require precision angles or shapes. Need a specific shape for a ball hopper using only bent angles? This can be achieved using a machine called a **press brake**. The press brake uses stored energy (mechanical, pneumatic, hydraulic, etc.) to produce the immense force necessary to bend metal. Most commonly used for plate or sheet metal, these machines use corresponding punches and dies to bend the material in specific places and at specified angles. A punch is a hardened metal tool that is used to press the material in the corner being bent. The punch is always on the interior of the bend. The die is effectively the hardened metal cavity that forms the exterior side of the bend. The punch effectively puts tons of pressure on a sheet of metal until it conforms to the shape of the die below. Using a variety of punch and die sets, machinists can perform a number of precise bending operations to shape sheets of metal.

Similar to the way in which sheet metal is bent precisely, there are also bending machines for metal tubes. Bent metal tubes can make great robot frames, claws, or armatures. Using tubular punches and dies, operators force the material into a desired angle. After completing one angle, operators can also bend the same tube in a different axis to get complex three-dimensional forms. Precision bending and welding together can make impressive and stable robot structures.

Soldering

This section applies to the construction of electronics and circuitry on the robot. Making good electrical connections is critical to a robot's reliable performance and operation. Soldering is used to create an electrical connection between wires or electrical components. This method uses an iron with a temperature of 420°F (215°C) and above to melt a solder material. The iron does not get hot enough to melt the metal components you are bonding, but it does need to reach a high enough temperature to have the solder flow through braided wire and onto a sufficient surface area of components.

In order to achieve good flow and melting temperature, solder also often uses a catalyst called flux. The flux can either

When soldering components onto the backside of a printed circuit board, make sure the solder tip stays clean.

be part of the soldering compound or in a separate reservoir, requiring that components be dipped in it before applying the iron. Always try to keep a clean solder tip and be wary of fumes produced by the soldering process. This work should be done in a well-ventilated area, ideally with a fume extractor placed next to the piece you're soldering.

SOLDERING TIP

Solder does melt at temperatures lower than required for a good flowing electrical connection. This is called a cold solder and needs to be avoided at all costs. So, make sure your iron reaches the right temperature before starting.

Putting Designs into Practice

So far in this chapter, we have outlined a number of standard manufacturing processes. Every different method can be effective in a huge range of applications. This section will focus on implementation of design using a number of these different methods. Using the same basic idea of a claw assembly, we will visit some possible manufacturing solutions. This should show your team that there is no single correct answer in the process of fabrication toward a design. Moreover, this section should reveal in many ways that expensive machine equipment isn't even necessary for the implementation of a good design. Let's get creative!

A Simple Claw Assembly

This design uses two identical plates with identical hole patterns to create each half of a claw. Using bolts to secure the plates to the aluminum spacers or standoffs, we can create depth for the claw to grasp around an object with better coverage. Note that this assembly is constructed out of raw materials without relying on a kit of parts. This claw is relatively simple in both design and assembly and is possible to manufacture with modest means.

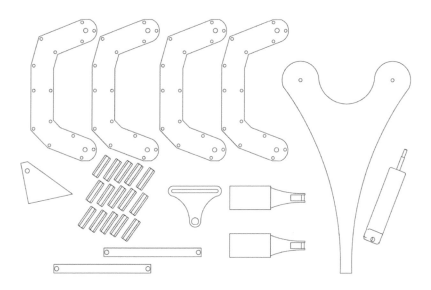

Two-dimensional drawings for the claw assembly were made before making the pieces was attempted.

The plates can be cut cleanly on a CNC router or mill with a large enough table. This may be the most efficient, but certainly not the only, means of fabricating these pieces. Notice that the critical part of the assembly is the alignment of the holes for the spacers or standoffs. How could this be done with just hand tools? To start, it may help to print out a template for the piece with specified locations for cutting and drilling operations that can be glued to the surface of the material. This step could also be done freehand for the first section of the claw. Once one section is done, trace around it with a sharpie or grease pencil. Cut out the same outline and you will have a second section that is roughly identical if done with a steady cutting hand. With the two sections cut out, clamp them together and sand or file the edges until they are flush with one another. You can then drill through both at the same time by anchoring them with a vice or set of clamps. This could be performed with a hand drill or on a drill press. You should always start by drilling a small hole initially before stepping up the size of the bit to make a cleaner cut and prevent the drill from drifting as you make the first hole.

Whether or not your team has access to professional engineering equipment, you should be able to find a method for producing quality pieces in a safe and effective way. We've already got the start of a good-looking claw mechanism. Let's move on to the pivot points of the claw that will eventually be connected to a motor or pneumatic shaft. The claw sections need either to have a fixed shaft which rotates in a bearing, or likewise, to have a set of bearings which fit around a fixed shaft at the pivot. Either way, we'll have to snugly fix a bearing or bearing-like assembly to a shaft for the crux of this mechanism.

One of the most straightforward ways to achieve this is by using a lathe to machine a precision shaft or tube for a bearing.

If the shaft or tube has the right tolerance of a few thousandths of an inch smaller or larger than a bearing, respectively, it will have what's known as a **press fit**. This means the bearing will not slide freely up and down the shaft, requiring some force for removal. This precision is achieved by using a cutting bit to

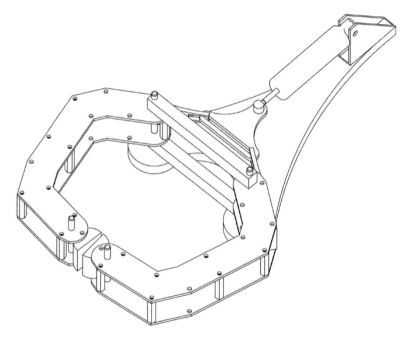

All of the pieces for the claw were assembled and modeled in CAD. This provides assurance the assembly will fit.

remove a few thousandths of an inch at a time. For a shaft, you can actually remove small amounts at a time by chucking the piece up into a drill press and carefully applying sandpaper to the spinning shaft. Use a caliper to measure how much material you've taken off the shaft after each round of sanding. This can be an effective way to get press fits on a tight budget.

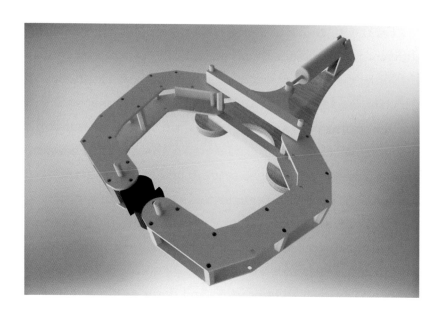

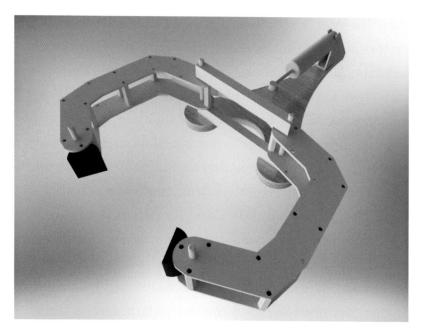

When the actuator is activated, the claw opens due to the linkage of the shaft and the pivots on the fingers.

For the inner diameter of a tube, the tooling is a bit different. Once the dimension is close to a desired press fit after the initial cutting tool, machinists use a tool called a **reamer**, which is like a precision drill bit. Using a large number of flutes, a reamer makes very fine and clean cuts to concentric inner diameters. Reamers can be used without a lathe, however. If your team has a drill press that can be run on low gear, reaming operations can be performed once the hole is close to the correct dimension. Alternatively, you can spin a reamer *by hand* into a piece of machinable plastic or even aluminum (warning: this may take a while).

After pairing a set of bearings and shafts or tubes, you're ready to attach collars to secure them to the frame of the claw. The shaft or tube will go in the holes we drilled at the pivot points, and you can secure the collars using setscrews. Setscrews are capless screws used to secure fixtures to round sections of pieces. If you made the shaft collars by hand, you will have to drill and tap the hole for a suitable setscrew. Taps cut threads into holes of corresponding size. Always use tap cutting fluid and occasionally turn the tap backwards to break chips off in the hole to prevent snags and tool breaks.

With the structure of the claw secured but rotating freely, we're ready to attach our motors or pneumatic actuators to the mechanism. If you chose a fixed shaft for the "grabbing" part of the claw, you can attach a sprocket to those shafts using another setscrew. Use two chains to attach the motors to the pivots and your claw will be picking up objects in no time.

With a pneumatic actuator, you'll want to have the tip of the actuator be able to rotate as well. For this, you can use bearings, but it won't be necessary for effective operation of the claw. You can really use any circular opening and a nut and bolt to ensure the captivity of the actuator shaft. After that, hook up your compressors or air tanks and begin testing pressures. Once you've calibrated the pneumatic system, you should be able to snatch up some points!

The louder the sound picked up by the microphone, the more voltage it will output. A microphone is an analog device.

5 Control Systems and Programming

In order to communicate with the motors, actuators, and other devices on the robot, your team will need to know how to speak robot. In essence, this means learning the content and syntax of a programming language to give the mechanisms clear messages on how to operate. In order to do this, you need to write and upload code to a device called a microcontroller. In this chapter, we'll go over the role of microcontrollers, a bit of programming theory, and how to use sensors to get better control on your robot. While we won't go in depth learning specific programming languages (there are many languages that are well equipped for controlling robots), we will tackle programming philosophies and practices that should help across any platform.

Microcontrollers are like the brains of the robot. These devices also serve as a kind of translator between your code and the mechanisms being controlled. In other words, motors and servos don't "understand" commands like "Go!" They respond when they are provided with voltage from a controller and a power source that makes the electromagnets move inside. The microcontroller's job is to take the information from its inputs (joystick, sensors, autonomous code, etc.) and output an electrical signal to an output device. Outputs from microcontrollers are usually low voltage analog or digital signals between 0 and 5VDC.

Analog and Digital

You may have heard the terms analog and digital with regards to electronics used in music. In a nutshell, the term analog refers to any mechanism in which changing physical states can be represented as data. In English, this means that analog devices measure something physically happening and convert that measurement into a useful medium like voltage. Let's use a microphone as an example. Microphones measure physical disturbances of air pressure caused by sound waves and convert those disturbances into small amounts of voltage. The louder the source of the sound, the more the microphone capsule will be affected, and the more voltage the microphone will output. Moreover, the output voltage of the microphone represents the continuous form of the incoming sound wave as it moves the capsule. **Analog signals** are all continuous, meaning they can give readings anywhere between two values along a sensor's range. This is important for understanding the input and output capabilities of your microcontroller. Analog devices are usually less susceptible to signal noise than digital ones and can give a better resolution in many cases.

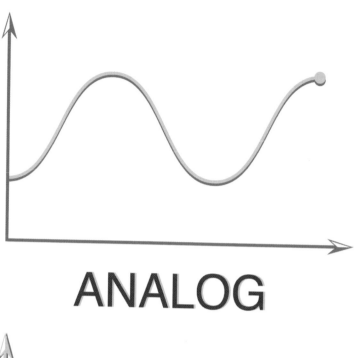

ANALOG

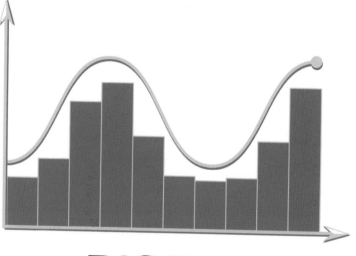

DIGITAL

These figures show how analog signals can be digitally represented or approximated using discrete values.

Digital inputs and outputs perform the same basic function of receiving and sending data to and from the microcontroller. **Digital signals** differ in a few important ways, though. While analog signals are continuous, digital signal processing (DSP) relies on breaking down information into discrete values. Discrete, here, means that there is a finite number of values which a digital signal can represent for a given input or output. In its most simple form, a digital signal can have two values. This is called a logic signal and can represent 1 and 0 or "on" and "off." You may have heard of binary code, which uses a series of 1's and 0's to perform computations. In fact, all code for computers and machines is based on logic signals.

Analog signals can also be *converted* into digital ones and vice-versa. Your robot's microcontroller is likely to have an ADC (analog to digital converter) as well as a DAC (digital to analog converter) available. So how does conversion work for an input or output device? Let's use the example of the microphone again. USB microphones are very common these days for capturing audio signals and converting them into digital signals for a computer or recording interface. In order to do this, they need to take the continuous, analog signal from the capsule and convert it into a discrete number of values. For audio signals, which are based on time, the ADC has to chop up the signal into sections in a process called sampling. Sampling a signal takes readings at a given interval in order to represent change over time. It is a kind of averaging process that captures the shape of an analog signal.

In the figures on pages 93 and 95, you can see how the digital signal approximates the shape of the analog frequency

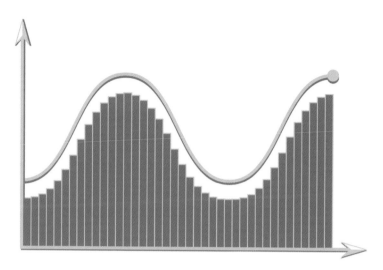

DIGITAL

With higher resolution, the digital signal more accurately models the analog response.

with a series of discrete voltages. The number of slices, or samples, over a given period of time is called the **sample rate** and will determine the accuracy of the representation. Some applications like high-quality audio production will require a sample rate of 44,100 samples per second or more to accurately represent an analog source. On the robot, the sample rate is called a baud rate. The baud rate determines how fast a digital input will gather discrete values and how many times a second the microcontroller can run computations in the code you write. This is important for understanding how the efficiency of your code and usage of digital devices can affect the speed of the robot executing commands from the microcontroller.

In the previous chapter, we went over pulse width modulation in relation to motor controllers. You can now begin to see how the digital pulse signal acts as a representation of linear voltage increases or decreases used to determine the speed of the motor. PWM is also an example of a logic signal because it only turns the motor on or off at a constant voltage.

For low voltage components like some servos, you can send a signal directly from the microcontroller to the servo and get it to operate. A servo is like a small motor that has the ability to sense position built in. This is especially handy when you need the robot to perform precise movements or you need to consistently perform the same motion. Servos achieve this by giving feedback to the microcontroller based on the position (in degrees) of the shaft relative to a starting point. This means that, as the shaft of the servo motor rotates, an analog device known as a potentiometer rotates with it, giving an input signal to the servo's control circuit. In order to communicate this information back to the microcontroller, the control circuit samples the reading from the potentiometer and outputs it as a digital signal as feedback for the controller to tell precisely how far it has rotated from a starting point. Many servos operate within a finite range of 180 degrees, which provides a logical starting point at either end of that range.

Servos can be one of the easiest places to start when learning how to code your robot. This is because you can easily see how the changes in degrees of a servo match up to the values you put into your program. In this section, we'll go over how to set up your microcontroller to output a PWM signal to one of your servos to get it moving. First, you'll need to connect the servo to the correct output pins on the microcontroller. On robotics controllers, there are usually specific servo outputs

SENSE OF DIRECTION

There are servos that can rotate indefinitely, like a normal motor. These are called "continuous rotation servos," and they operate a bit differently. Potentiometers in normal servos have a physical range over which they can rotate. This makes them ideal candidates for the feedback device. In order to escape this limitation, continuous rotation servos use digital devices called "**rotary encoders.**" Rotary encoders use a light sensor to detect a light source through a series of holes in a rotating disc. If a hole moves over the light sensor, it will produce a logic signal of 1 or "on" as an input to the encoder's control circuit. When the space in between two holes blocks the light from reaching the sensor, the signal reads "off." This makes it so the encoder can count up the number of times it receives on and off signals from the light sensor to determine how far the wheel has rotated. Given that the holes are spaced at regular intervals, the encoders use the change from an off state to an on state to represent degrees of rotation. Even more useful still, the circuit can calculate how many times per second the state of the light sensor changes, giving the robot accurate feedback on how fast the motors are actually running.

If the encoder receives signals only from the light sensor turning on and off, then how can it tell which direction the motor is running? If it were to run backward, you would be receiving a stream of 1's and 0's the same as you would when spinning the motor forward. In order to tackle this problem, rotary encoders actually have two light sensors. Each light sensor has a corresponding set of holes in the spinning disc that is different from the other. This makes it so the pattern of light sensors turning on and off is unique for each direction. In other words, the control circuit can tell if the reading from the two sensors is following the "forward" or "reverse" pattern by comparing it to the previous feedback value.

with three pins for each servo cable. These three pins, or headers, provide grounding, power, and signal to the servo. The cable on the servo should reflect this order as well, with the ground wire (usually black or brown), the power wire (usually red), and the signal wire (usually yellow or white). Be sure to make note of which number output you put the servo in because we'll need to reflect that in our code.

With the servo hooked up, we can start defining, for our microcontroller, the various pieces we're using in the code. In order for the controller to run a program, it has to know

A servo is hooked up to an Arduino microcontroller with the three pins for each servo cable.

which inputs and outputs to receive and send information from. Moreover, the controller has to know what code protocol will be used in order to use certain devices. For instance, when using a servo, you will usually have to import a servo library, which makes it easier to control in the code. The servo library allows you to identify rotations in terms of degrees based on the feedback from the servo's control circuit. Without the library, you would have to do the legwork of reading the output from the servo's signal pin, then issuing motor commands in terms of a manual PWM signal. You can save yourself the trouble with the library and tell the microcontroller to set a specific position like 90 degrees.

Simple Script

The following example "code" isn't written in any particular language but is here to help you understand the process of setting up a simple script. Note that any line starting with "//" denotes a "comment" or piece of code that is not executable in the program. We'll go more in depth with comments later, but here they will act as markers to show you what's at play in each part of the program.

The example code on page 100 shows a bit of the process of setting up a device to be operated by the microcontroller. Notice how everything is spelled out, even if it seems obvious that, for example, we have the servo plugged in. Every code needs to be set up methodically enough for a computer with no prior knowledge of your system to be able to operate it. Imagine if you were asked to help someone who had never

```
//Import the servo library for use in this program
import <servo.lib>

//Identify your servo(s) that will be used in the program
servo = "SweepyTheServo" //You can call it whatever you want

//Give the microcontroller a variable to store the servo's position
define (Position; 0) //The zero provides a blank slate for the
controller's memory

setup {
        //Let the controller know which pin you plugged the
        servo into
        SweepyTheServo.Pin(Servo1)
        //Identify setup protocol from the program
        } //The setup is contained in the brackets

//Begin the executable part of the program
run.program(loop) {
                SweepyTheServo.write(Position,50); //"Write" the
                command to the servo pin
                wait(100ms); //Pause the servo for 100 milliseconds
                SweepyTheServo.write(Position,100); //Move the
                servo to 100 degrees from start
                wait(150ms); //Observe slightly longer pause
                SweepyTheServo.write(Position,25); //Move the
                servo in the opposite direction
                wait(300ms);

        } //The program then moves back to where the loop
        began and runs infinitely
```

*A bit of sample code showing some syntax and commenting techniques.
Make sure to keep your code documented.*

even heard of a sandwich to make a PB&J. You may very well be able to assume that they know what bread, peanut butter, and jelly are (import the "FoodsInThePantry" library to this example). You would have to start out in a similar way, outlining all of the individual ingredients before spreading them with the knife. Only after they had assembled all the ingredients (define(Peanut Butter); Knife = "ButterKnife"; etc.) could you begin walking them through the steps of your recipe. The recipe would then move in a linear fashion through all the steps before the sandwich-making process ends. However, if the steps of the recipe were a loop like our example program, you would end up making infinite sandwiches. Let's go over a few of the ways to write programs with more complex results.

Printing and Debugging

When writing and testing your code, the response of the robot's motors or servos shouldn't be the only thing you can observe about how your program works. As such, you will need to read what your microcontroller is getting as an input as well as what it's producing as an output. You can achieve this by "**printing**" values from your code. These will show up on the computer. A "Print" operation is usually called after a line that produces a value that's useful to the program. Printing takes the value of a given input or output and converts it into a readable text format for the programmer. For instance, if you have a tension gauge as an input, you'll want to get the reading from that gauge, then print the reading so you can see what you're working with. Let's look at the example on page 102.

```
setup {
        //Let the controller know which pin the tension gauge
        is on
        TensionGauge.Pin(pin1);
        }

//Begin the executable part of the program
run.program(loop) {
        //Get the value of the voltage from the tension gauge
        readAnalog(TensionGauge);
        //Print the value from the pin
        print("Tension  :  (TensionGauge)");
        //Make a new line for every new value for easy
        reading
print.newLine;
                }
```

Printing helps to keep track of what your code is doing when it runs.

As you can see, the printing process will return information to you in a structure that you set up yourself. Without identifying "Tension : (TensionGauge)", you would just have a stream of numbers. Being thorough with printing allows you to know exactly what each value is and where it came from on the robot. This is valuable especially when you have a lot of analog and digital readings in your program and you need to tell what's happening to each of them. Effectively, printing will allow you to be able to tell if your code is getting the values you expect, as well as performing the operations you intend.

CLEAN MACHINE

"Debugging" is a term used to describe the process of hunting down errors in a program or testing code to improve function by changing values where necessary. This term originates from the early days of computing when a famous computer scientist named Grace Murray Hopper was troubleshooting a problem on a new system. When Admiral Hopper opened the computer, she found a moth stuck in an electrical component, which was causing the unit to fail. When you're debugging a piece of code, think of it like pulling out all the metaphorical "moths" in the program to make it function as intended.

Admiral Grace Murray Hopper was one of the most important programmers of the twentieth century..

With a Print command after every valuable reading or operation, you will have all the information you need to troubleshoot, or "debug," the robot.

A Few Basic Operators

The microcontroller will always move linearly through the commands you write in a program. Knowing this can help us come up with creative ways to use common programming operators. An **"If Then" statement** is perhaps the most common and most fundamental operator in robotics. This operator does exactly what it sounds like, checking to see if a condition is met, and if so, performing an action. For example, "If" you press the button on the joystick, "Then" the robot's winch motor spins for five seconds. These statements will occupy a majority of your code strategy insofar as you'll be thinking of the ways you can get readings from your sensors, then use those readings to control the robot.

Many If Then statements are paired with a corresponding **"Else" statement** or **"Else If" statement.** If a condition of an If Then statement is not met, an "Else" can provide an alternative operation for the code to execute. This operator rather literally could translate in English to something like: "If the robot picks up a ball, we will score it. Otherwise (Else) the robot will drive around to play defense." When an If Then is not paired with another statement like Else, it only represents one new operation for the robot. This means that the state of the robot will only change if the "If" condition is met. The "Else If" statement has the ability of giving more than two

A robot uses control logic to place the ball in a goal after getting into position.

sets of possible operations. This is very useful for situations where you might have a few possible outcomes for a statement or reading from a sensor. For instance, you might need to have three different positions for a claw based on what a color sensor sees. In English, that would be something like "If the robot sees red, raise the claw halfway. Else if the robot sees blue, raise the claw three-quarters of the way. Otherwise, if the sensor sees yellow, raise the claw all the way up."

A **"While" loop** is a lot like an "If Then" statement in that it checks to see if a condition is met. However, a While loop is a bit more specialized in that it continues to execute the loop as long as the condition is satisfied. As an example, the robot's winch motor will spin "While" you hold down the button on the joystick, giving you a bit more control for some applications. When you let go of the button, the controller will "exit" the While loop and continue moving straight down the script.

"For" loops are like While loops but are a bit more specific. These loops require a variable, a test condition, and an increment. This means that the For loop takes an input, checks to see if that input is within a specified range or quantity, then applies an incremental change to that input. For loops usually operate until the incremental increase or decrease of a value exceeds the range of the test condition. In terms of practical applications, For loops are used for mechanisms that have a desired threshold as well as a desired time it takes to reach that threshold. The most common example may be using a For loop to make the robot's drivetrain accelerate until it hits a certain speed when given a command from the joystick.

Similar to regular language, programming uses conjunctions to create specific conditions in statements. The operator "And" works just like it would in any normal sentence

A small camera at the top of the shooter lines up the shot before firing the ball into a goal.

and is often used to modify other statements. For instance, you could have an If statement that requires two or more conditions to be true. "If the compressor is charged *And* there is a ball in the shooter, *And* the camera is locked on, Then the shooter will release the ball."

Where the "And" operator requires multiple conditions to be true in an If statement, you can use the conjunction "Or" to set up a different operation. "Or" operators make it so there could be more than one condition that would satisfy an If statement for the robot. For example: "If the robot's touch sensor is pressed, *Or* the color sensor sees blue, Then the lever will deploy." That way, only one statement must be true to be able to perform the consequent action. These conjunctions are very useful for controlling parts of the robot that have both manual and autonomous capabilities.

EASY DOES IT

Increment and Decrement functions are great for creating acceleration curves for motors, which can increase control and stability of the robot.

Math Operators and Functions

Now that we've gone over a few of the operators used to structure a program, let's talk a bit about the math behind programming a robot. In every language used for programming robots, mathematical operators are critical for calculating acceleration curves for motors, dynamic responses to sensors, and much more. Many of these tasks are performed with very basic operations like addition (+), subtraction (–), multiplication (*), and division(/). All of these operators function exactly as you'd expect them to when crunching numbers in a math class. The operator "Modulo" (%) is used to calculate a remainder if you need to output integer values from an operation. There are also operators which make comparisons between values like less than (<), greater than (>), equal to (– –), not equal to (!–), less than or equal to (<–), and greater than or equal to (>–). Different languages may notate these differently, but they should all be available to you when writing your code. Note that the "equal to" symbol here does not match the usual (=) symbol. This is because that symbol is usually used to perform a definition function as seen in the examples above.

Some of the more useful and interesting mathematical functions are the Increment (i++) and Decrement (i– –) operators. These take a value and add or subtract over time as the program runs. You can understand these operations as being equivalent to $(i = I + 1)$ and $(i = I - 1)$ respectively. This means that the function will return a value larger every time the function is called. In a loop, for instance, the increment function will add 1 to the value "i" every time the loop comes back around. They are often used in conjunction with For loops.

With just these tools, you can tackle very complicated problems with the code on your robot. Let's take a look at how these operators can work for a problem like smoothing out the movement of a robotic arm. For this example, we'll be programming an acceleration and deceleration curve to the motor controlling the arm to make it less jerky when moving from a rest position and reaching its desired position. We'll use a motor encoder as an input for the position of the arm.

The code on pages 110 and 111 has three different possible operations based on the position of the robot's arm as it moves. It creates an incremental acceleration if the trigger on the

```
setup {
        //Let the controller know which pin the encoder and
        motor are on
        ArmPosition.Pin(pin1);
        MotorPWM.Pin(pin5);
        //Identify an input from the controller
        ArmButton.Map(RightTrigger);
        ArmButton.Pin(pin2);
        }


//Begin the executable part of the program
run.program(loop) {
        //Get the value of the voltage from the tension gauge
        readDigital(ArmPosition);
        //Print the value from the pin
        print("Degrees : (ArmPosition)");
        //Make a new line for every new value for easy reading
        print.newLine;
        //Create While statement for pulling the trigger on the
        controller
        while(ArmButton = true){
                //Set up an increment to accelerate
                for(i = 0, ArmPosition<80, i++){
                        writeDigital(MotorPWM, i);
                        wait(10ms); //Make the acceleration
                        gradual in 10ms intervals
                        }
        //Create a deceleration curve when the arm passes
        a midpoint
                for(i = 0, ArmPosition>-80 And <165, i--){
                        writeDigital(MotorPWM, i);
                        wait(10ms); //Make the deceleration
                        gradual in 10ms intervals
                        }
```

```
        //When the arm reaches its final position, stop
        the motor
        if(ArmPosition>–165){
                writeDigital(MotorPWM, 0);
                }
        }
}
```

A bit of sample code showing how to use feedback from sensors to increase control of a robotic arm.

controller is held until the motor encoder shows that the arm is halfway to its desired position of 165 degrees. When the arm passes the halfway point, the acceleration will decrease until it hits the 165-degree mark, at which point the motor turns off. This will prevent the arm from overextending and from jerking to a single speed from a rest position.

PID Loops and Finer Control

Sometimes, the robot will need to use readings from sensors and consequent outputs to motors to achieve tasks that have a low margin for error. If the robot needs to press a very small button without hitting other pieces around it, you will have to make sure that any error in the path gets corrected before the button is pressed. **PID loops** offer a very interesting solution to problems like this as they calculate error over time from sensors and compensate with corresponding outputs. This means that the loop will check to see how far off a sensor's value is from a desired reading as well as how long this margin of error has persisted. If the error persists over a longer period of time, then the loop outputs a more drastic command to a motor or mechanism that is used to correct that error.

The "P" stands for "proportion" and represents the current value that's been gathered by the PID loop. The "I" is for "integral" and looks at a collection of past values to compare to the new value. The "D" calculates expected future values known as the "derivative" based on the rate of change from older values to new ones. In a nutshell, a PID loop is set up to gather information over time and compensate for undesirable trends in that information. They are used frequently for applications in which the robot is likely to under- and overshoot a desired position or state.

Two light sensors are used to read the difference between the surface of the table and the black line between them.

One of the best examples is getting a robot to follow a line using two light sensors. If the light sensors are positioned on the outer edges a line, they can be used to detect the difference in reflection between the line of tape and the floor on both sides of the line. The robot will have a desired state of seeing only the reflection of the line from both sensors and will send a command to the motors to simply drive forward. If the left sensor sees the line but the right sensor sees the floor, the PID loop will output a command to the drivetrain to spin the motors on the right side of the drivetrain, causing movement to the left. If the robot is not turning fast enough, the right-side light sensor will continue to give undesirable readings to the PID loop over time. This will make the PID loop steadily increase the turn rate until the robot gets back on track with both sensors reading the line. A PID loop is much more finely tuned than a simple set of If Else statements in this application because it responds to change over time instead of simply taking the most recent reading from the sensors.

Conclusion

Programming and controlling a robot is certainly an exercise in logic, mathematics, and creativity. Now that we have gone over a brief overview of programming practices and common operators in robotics, your team should be able to sit down and take a stab at getting a few systems up and running. The programming process will involve a lot of trial and error, so don't be discouraged when things don't work as intended the first time. Part of the fun of programming is conquering complex problems by coming up with innovative ways to use various operators and functions together. It's good to experiment and tweak the code until the robot feels good to drive and score points.

Your team will save lots of time and many headaches if you exhibit good programming strategies. Code that is clearly written and well documented can only help you when it comes to debugging or editing later. Diligent use of comments and printing will help you to keep your place in a dense program and make it easier to navigate. If you follow a few of the steps outlined in this chapter, your robot will be that much closer to coming to life and competing with the best of them. After the programming is complete, you can really take a step back and be amazed at how it all comes together. The motors will spin, the claw will grasp, and the sensors will collect great information. This moving mass of metal and electronics is a great achievement for your team, and you can show it proudly to your community as a testament to your knowledge, hard work, and dedication.

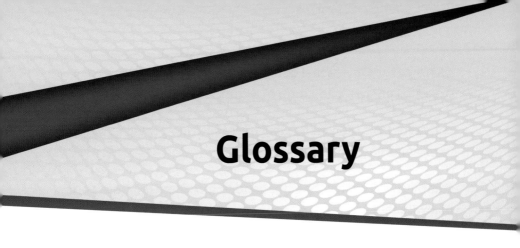

Glossary

amperage Rate of electron flow through a circuit per second; measured in amperes.

analog signal Continuous signal in which a changing physical variable is represented over time as a voltage.

Anderson Power Poles Colorful plastic connectors that connect two wires by snapping together.

AWG American Wire Gauge scale; used to measure the cross-sectional diameter and number of strands in a wire.

CAD Computer-aided design, which uses a two- or three-dimensional drawing environment to represent the design of physical objects.

center of gravity Center point of the distributed mass of the robot in which the weight is balanced.

CNC Computer numerical control for machines to execute cutting patterns or perform precision operations based on a programmed tool path.

compressor Device that converts power from a motor into potential energy in the form of a compressed air cylinder.

conveyor belt Mechanism that uses tensioned rotating belts to move objects in a linear direction.

crimping To add a connector used to terminate the bare ends of a wire that promotes connectivity and reliable connections.

dead short Direct, unmitigated connection between positive and negative terminals in an electric circuit.

digital signal Electrical signal comprised of bits of discrete voltages that represent information.

duty cycle The percentage of time in which a PWM signal is in the "on" state for a single period.

elevator lift Mechanism that uses a fixed endpoint on a chain or belt to raise or lower an object with a motor.

"Else If" statement A set of alternative commands, each with its own conditions, which are executed if a higher level condition is not met.

"Else" statement An alternative command issued when a given condition is not satisfied.

extrusion The operation that gives a two–dimensional drawing the depth of a third dimension in CAD software.

ferrule crimp Connector used for inserting wires into screw terminals.

finite element analysis Computer simulation for the strength of a design under various conditions like heat, pressure, and vibration.

foot-pound Measurement of force required to move 1 pound a distance of 1 foot.

"For" loop A loop with an iterative (involving repetition) process that changes the value of a variable each time the loop is executed.

fuse Electrical device that stops the flow of electricity through a circuit when a threshold amperage or voltage is exceeded.

gear ratio The speed of a gear's rotation relative to the rotation of a connected gear expressed as a ratio.

glass transition temperature The temperature at which a material like ABS plastic begins to deform or become malleable.

"If Then" statement A command that is executed when a given condition is satisfied.

lathe A machine that rotates a part for a cutting tool which can move in the x and y axes.

mentor Experienced volunteer dedicated to educating and helping students during the robotics season and beyond.

microcontroller A control circuit with onboard memory and programmable inputs and outputs.

milling machine A fabrication machine with a high-RPM spindle and a bed that moves in three axes.

PID loop Proportional-integral-derivative controller, which takes feedback from a sensor and compensates for error over time by adjusting the output response of the loop.

pneumatic actuator Mechanism that converts compressed air into linear motion using a piston in a sealed chamber.

power Rate of energy consumed by a circuit over time; measured in watts.

press brake Machine used to precisely bend sheet metal at various angles.

press fit Mechanical tolerance that requires significant force to overcome the friction between a part and an inserted object.

printing The process of converting digital or analog information from a microcontroller into readable text for a programmer.

PSI Pounds per square inch is a unit of measurement to denote the pressure of 1 pound on an area of 1 square inch.

pulse width modulation A signal in which information is transferred or power is supplied using a series of electrical on/off pulses at varying durations and intervals.

quick connects Bladed connectors used between wires or for circuit breakers and fuses.

rack and pinion Gear-driven assembly that converts rotational motion into linear motion using a flat section of teeth.

reamer Tool for boring holes to precision diameters.

resistance Relative difficulty for electricity to pass through a given circuit; measured in ohms.

ring terminal Crimp with a circular conductor used for connecting to bolts or posts.

robot technician General worker and fabricator for a robotics team.

rotary encoder A device that uses light sensors and a perforated wheel to calculate speed and direction of a shaft.

rotating brush collector A mechanism that uses a spinning set of bristles to move game pieces on the floor into a robot.

sample rate Frequency at which a signal is converted into bits for digital signal processing.

scissor lift Assembly with multiple repeating X pattern stages that lifts proportionally to the movement of the first stage.

slip fit Mechanical tolerance that allows for movement between a part and an inserted object.

soldering Process that forms an electrical connection between two conductors by heating a metal filler material until it flows between the wires or terminals.

solder sleeve Connection that uses a combination of heat shrink and solder to form an electrical connection between wires.

solenoid A device that uses an electrical signal to open and close a valve.

spring launcher A device that uses a compression spring to store potential energy for a piston to fire a projectile.

3-D printer A device that creates three-dimensional objects by extruding thin layers on top of one another over time to create depth.

torque The force of a rotating object around a center point such as a motor shaft.

voltage Potential difference of electrons between two terminals of a circuit measured in volts.

welding Joining process of two metals (or thermoplastics) using fusion to melt the base materials together in conjunction with an added filler metal.

"While" loop A loop that operates as long as a given condition is met.

winch Mechanism that winds cable or rope on or off a spool to create a desired lift or tension.

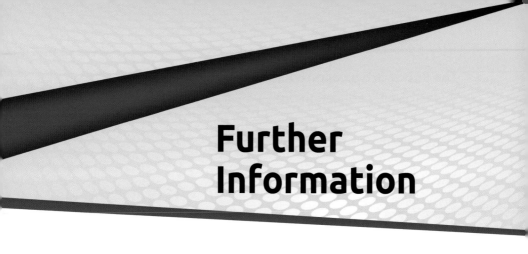

Further Information

Competition Websites

Botball

www.botball.org
Botball is a competitive robotics platform for autonomous robots only. Botball robots utilize the C programming language to perform their autonomous runs.

FIRST Robotics

www.firstinspires.org
This site is the clearinghouse for all FIRST competitions from Jr. FLL to FRC. You can find rules, registration, and area event information here.

NASA

www.nasa.gov/offices/education/centers/kennedy/
technology/nasarmc/about
This competition is for college-level students, but can be a good resource for seeing what the next step looks like. Held at the Kennedy Space Center, the competition features robots digging up and collecting various kinds of dirt and rock to simulate an extraterrestrial environment

The Robotics Education Foundation

www.roboticseducation.org

The Robotics Education Foundation provides two separate competitions for VEX IQ and VEX EDR robots.

The World Robot Olympiad

www.wroboto.org

The World Robot Olympiad is a yearly competition that has dance, football (soccer), and search and rescue categories.

Instructional Websites

Chief Delphi

www.chiefdelphi.com

These forums are a great resource to connect with other FIRST robotics teams. There is also a lot of useful information for general robotics, design, and programming.

GitHub

github.com

GitHub is a collaboration tool for the programming and web design team. The site allows you to upload and work on code in various languages without altering the format. Use this tool to divide up different programming tasks and conquer!

GrabCAD

grabcad.com

GrabCAD is an open-source library of two-dimensional and three-dimensional drawings and files. Need a model of a part you don't know how to measure for your robot assembly? You can probably find something like it to start with on this site.

Instructables

www.instructables.com

A haven for all things DIY, Instructables provides a place for users to show off their projects with step-by-step breakdowns. Can be very useful when looking for inspiration on how to tackle a new project.

Make Magazine

www.youtube.com/user/makemagazine/
playlists?sort=dd&view=1

Make Magazine has a very active YouTube channel with tons of interesting content. In particular, the "Colin's Lab" series of videos can teach you a lot about circuits.

MIT

ocw.mit.edu/index.htm

The Massachusetts Institute of Technology offers free courses online in a huge range of fields. While definitely for the ambitious student, these courses present immense amounts of useful theory for robotics applications.

Pneumatics Online

www.pneumaticsonline.com/calculator.htm

This website is great for calculating requirements for pneumatic cylinders and actuators on your robot. The calculator can also be used to check your work after doing the calculations by hand in the shop.

Robot in 3 Days

www.youtube.com/user/robotin3days

The Robot in 3 Days YouTube channel shows what it's like to condense an entire robotics season into three short days.

Sparkfun

www.sparkfun.com

This website is great for getting into circuits or finding electronics and sensors for your robot.

Thang010146

www.youtube.com/user/thang010146

Thang010146 is a very straightforward but inspiring YouTube channel. This user makes animations of different CAD designs to showcase possible mechanisms.

Product Websites

DigiKey

www.digikey.com

DigiKey is an online electronics superstore. If you're building circuits and need resistors, capacitors, transistors, etc., DigiKey is good for getting what you need quick. They have a mind-numbing number of components, so try not to get lost!

McMaster-Carr

www.mcmaster.com

McMaster-Carr is a huge supplier of all things fabrication and manufacturing. This site is good for looking up off-the-shelf odds and ends or even for purchasing raw materials.

VEX Robotics

www.vexrobotics.com

VEX also has a robotic system of modular building parts for ease of construction. They sell both kits and parts for competition robots.

Index

About the Author

Kevin McCombs works as a research and development technician at a drone company based in Jacksonville, Florida. He has a bachelor's degree from New College of Florida in philosophy and music. With ten years' experience building competition robots, he is a mentor and volunteer at his brother's non-profit, which expands youth robotics in north Florida. The organization has facilitated the growth of more than 150 robotics teams in the area, with the hopes of putting a team in every public school. In his free time, when he isn't making machines and circuits, Kevin plays lead guitar in a death metal band and works as a mixing engineer for local music groups. Whether it's robotics or music, Kevin just likes working with metal.